Called to Build a More Fraternal and Evangelical World

SFO Resource Library

Called to Build a More Fraternal and Evangelical World

A CONCORDANCE TO THE SFO RULE

Benet A. Fonck, OFM

Franciscan Press
Quincy University

Called to Build a More Fraternal and Evangelical World
Benet A. Fonck, OFM

Franciscan Press
Quincy University
1800 College Avenue
Quincy, IL 62301
PH 217.228.5670
FAX 217.228.5672
http://www.qufranciscanpress.com

Book design and typesetting by Laurel Fitch, Chicago, IL.
Cover design by Laurel Fitch

Printed in the United States of America
First Edition: 2002
First Printing: 2002
1 2 3 4 5 6 7 8 9 0

Library of Congress Cataloguing-in-Publication Data
Fonck, Benet A.
    Called to build a more fraternal and evangelical world: a concordance to the
SFO rule / Benet A. Fonck
        p. cm. — (SFO resource library ; 6)
    Includes bibliographical references and index.
    ISBN 0-8199-0991-2
    1. Secular Franciscan Order--Rules. 2. Secular Franciscan Order. Regula Ordinis
Franciscani Saecularis. I. Title. II. Series.

BX3654.F66 2001
255'.3--dc32   99-055295

Permissions

Excerpts from *The Jerusalem Bible*, copyright (c) 1966 by Random House/Doubleday
    and Company, Inc., Garden CIty, New York. Used with verbal permission.

Excerpts taken from *The Grail Psalmody*, copyright (c) 1966 by Ladies of the Grail
    (England). Used by permission of GIA Publications, Inc., Chicago, Illinois, exclusive
    agent. All rights reserved. Used with permission.

Excerpts from *Francis and Clare: The Complete Works*, trans. by Regis J. Armsrong,
    OFM Cap. and Ignatius C. Bardy, OFM; copyright (c) 1982 by The Missionary Society
    of St. Paul the Apostle in the State of New York. Used with permission of Paulist
    Press.

Excerpts from the English translation of *The Roman Missal* (c) 1973, International
    Committee on English in the Liturgy, Inc. All rights reserved.

Contents

T

Introduction

T The Rule of the Secular Franciscan Order is like a fine and sturdy home. Within its confines lives a healthy and dynamic family with its many experiences and expressions. It is built upon a solid foundation. It displays a distinctive architecture. It is situated within the context of a particular "neighborhood" with its complex of other dwellings.

Those who live within this rule of life are the Secular Franciscans around the world. Its foundations are the Sacred Scriptures, particular the holy Gospels, and the teachings and traditions of the Church. Its architecture is characterized by the legacy of St. Francis and St. Clare of Assisi and the heritage of the Franciscan sources. Its ambiance is the contemporary ecclesial community which is given particular shape by the documents of Vatican II and the thoughts of the recent Popes and also is given a special beauty through its liturgical expression captured in the prayers of the Church.

To fully appreciate a well built and artistic house, more than the building materials need to be examined. In like manner, to understand this rule, it is to be seen not just as an isolated text of beautiful ideas and finely turned phrases, but rather in the situation of its total environment. Because the Rule of the Secular Franciscan Order, as a way of life or a project for living, is the description of a life experience, the summary of an ideal, and the synthesis of almost eight hundred years of history for a spiritual family in an ecclesial culture, it needs to be studied, loved, and lived within the context of its spiritual roots, its resonance with the Gospel and with the Church, and its ramifications for daily living.

For this reason, a concordance of the Rule of the Secular, Franciscan Order, has been developed. For each of the twenty-six articles of the rule and its conclusion, ten corresponding quotes have been selected in order to give a well rounded picture of that text's intent and implications: from the Gospels, the New Testament, the Old Testament, the Psalms, the writings of St. Francis, the writing of St. Clare, the early Franciscan Sources, the documents of Vatican II, the writings of the recent Supreme Pontiffs, and finally a prayer from the Roman Missal. For each collection of citations, a particular theme was chosen to coordinate or highlight that aspect of that article of the rule.

The original idea for this concordance grew out of two experiences: the worthwhile value of a text compiled by Herbert Roggen, OFM which collected quotes of Francis and the Franciscan sources around particular themes (it is entitled *Spirit and Life*) and of a similar text put together for the sisters of the Franciscan Missionaries of Divine Motherhood, and the constant expressed need by Secular Franciscans (particularly the formation directors) and their spiritual assistants for something more than a commentary on the rule—a contextual study of the origins and orientations of this valuable way of life.

The actual selection of quotes has grown out of a collaboration of over twenty-five years with members of the Secular Franciscan Order and with the friars who attend to their pastoral and fraternal care: listening to them, praying with them, discussing with them, preaching for them has provided the insight and the judgment to see a certain article of the SFO Rule from a particular perspective.

The research for the various choices was stretched out over a period of more than ten years, but actually the project is not exhausted. In fact, it has only begun! For as many quotes that can be given to underline a special theme, just as many can be produced to emphasis other key ideas contained in the articles of the SFO Rule. It is hoped, then, that this is the first of many such concordances of the Rule of the Secular Franciscan Order.

The project of compiling this text has many aims: it is intended for directors of initial formation to help give the candidates a well rounded perspective on the way of life they are embracing. It is meant for coordinators of ongoing formation and continuing education within a fraternity to provide the materials for an in-depth study on a particular aspect of the rule. It could be used by the spiritual assistant in preparing conferences and homilies. It can be a help to the fraternity's liturgy team when planning a particular celebration or ceremony. It should also serve as a resource text for the fraternity council to allow it to understand more fully its responsibility to animate and guide the community in all dimension of its lived gospel vocation and its living Franciscan experience.

And, mainly, it is hoped that it would be a personal companion text for every Secular Franciscan to help him or her "encounter the living and active person of Christ" (Art. 5) in all aspects of life. This companion, in turn, would aid in forming an evangelical, ecclesial, apostolic, and Franciscan value system which will fulfill the Secular Franciscan's life and mission in the Church and in the world. This life and mission, lived out in a practical way day in and day out, would ultimately be able to "build a more fraternal and evangelical world so that the kingdom of God may be brought about more effectively" (Art. 14).

Benet A. Fonck, OFM

Abbreviations

T Writings of Francis: (pages in Armstrong/Brady)

Writings of Clare: (pages in Armstrong/Brady)

4L	*Fourth Letter to Agnes of Prague* (203)
5L	*Letter to Ermentrude of Bruges* (207)
RCl	*Rule of St. Clare* (209)
TCl	*Testament of St. Clare* (226)
BCl	*Blessing Attributed to St. Clare* (233)

Franciscan Sources: (pages in Omnibus of Sources)

1Cel	*First Life of Francis by Celano* (225)
2Cel	*Second Life of Francis of Celano* (357)
LM	*Major Life of Francis by Bonaventure* (629)
3Soc	*Legend of the Three Companions* (853)
LP	*Legend of Perugia* (957)
SF	*Mirror of Perfection* (1103)
3Stig	*3rd Consideration on the Stigmata* (1444)

Vatican II Documents: (pages in Flannery Edition)

SC	*Sacrosanctum Concilium* (Liturgy) (1)
LG	*Lumen Gentium (The Church)* (350)
UR	*Unitatis Redintegratio (Ecumenism)* (452)
PC	*Perfectae Caritatis (Religious Life)* (611)
AA	*Apostolicam Actuositatem (Laity)* (766)
AG	*Ad Gentes (Missions)* (813)
PO	*Presbyterorum Ordinis (Priests)* (863)
GS	*Gaudium et Spes (The Church Today)* (903)

Papal Statements:

PT	*Pacem in Terris (Peace on Earth)*, John XXIII
ES	*Ecclesiam Suam (Church)*, Paul VI
PP	*Populorum Progressio (Development of Peoples)*, Paul VI
EN	*Evangelii Nuntiandi (Evangelization)*, Paul VI
ET	*Evangelica Testificatio (Religious Life)*, Paul VI
RH	*Redemptor Hominis (Redeemer of Man)*, John Paul II
LB	*Laborem Exercens (Human Work)*, John Paul II
DM	*Dives in Misericordia (Mercy)*, John Paul II
FC	*Familiaris Corsortio (Christian Family)*, John Paul II
SD	*Salvifici Doloris (Human Suffering)*, John Paul II
RD	*Redemptionis Donum (Religious Consecration)*, John Paul II

SF   Exhortation to SFO Congress 1982, John Paul II
MX   Pope John Paul II in Mexico
JP   Speeches of John Paul I

chapter one

The Secular Franciscan Order (SFO)

Article 1

The Franciscan Family, as one among many spiritual families raised up by the Holy Spirit in the Church, unites all members of the people of God—laity, religious, and priests—who recognize that they are called to follow Christ in the footsteps of Saint Francis of Assisi.

In various ways and forms, but in life-giving union with each other, they intend to make present the charism of their common Seraphic Father in the life and mission of the Church.

THEME: CALL OF THE SPIRIT TO BE EVANGELIZED AND TO EVANGELIZE

GOSPEL: LK 4:1, 14–21

Filled with the Holy Spirit, Jesus left the Jordan and was led by the Spirit through the wilderness.

Jesus, with the power of the Spirit in him, returned to Galilee, and his reputation spread throughout the countryside. He taught in their synagogues and everyone praised him.

He came to Nazareth, where he had been brought up, and went into the synagogue on the sabbath day as he usually did. He stood up to read and they handed him the scroll of the prophet Isaiah. Unrolling the scroll he found the place where it is written:

> The spirit of the Lord has been given to me,
> for he has anointed me.
> He has sent me to bring the good news to the poor
> to proclaim liberty to captives
> and to the blind new sight,
> to set the downtrodden free,
> to proclaim the Lord's year of favor.

He then rolled up the scroll, gave it back to the assistant and sat down. And all eyes in the synagogue were fixed on him. Then he began to speak to them, "This text is being fulfilled today even as you listen."

NEW TESTAMENT: 1 THES 4:3,7

What God wants is for you all to be holy.... We have been called by God to be holy, not to be immoral; in other words, anyone who objects is not objecting to a human authority, but to God, who gave you his Holy Spirit.

also 1 Cor 1:26–31
    Eph 1:11–14

OLD TESTAMENT: JER 1:4–10,17–19

> The word of Yahweh was addressed to me, saying,
> "Before I formed you in the womb I knew you,
> before you came to birth I consecrated you;
> I have appointed you as prophet to the nations."
> I said, "Ah, Lord Yahweh, look, I do not know how to speak:
> I am a child!"
>
> But Yahweh replied,
> "Do not say, 'I am a child.'
> Go now to those to whom I send you

and say whatever I command you.
Do not be afraid of them,
for I am with you to protect you—
it is Yahweh who speaks."

Then Yahweh put out his hand and touched my mouth
        and said to me:
"There! I am putting my words into your mouth.
Look, today I am setting you
over nations and over kingdoms,
to tear up and to knock down,
to destroy and to overthrow,
to build and to plant.
So now brace yourself for action.
Stand up and tell them
all I command you.
Do not be dismayed at their presence,
or in their presence I will make you dismayed.
I, for my part, today will make you
into a fortified city,
a pillar of iron,
and a wall of bronze
to confront all this land:
the kings of Judah, its princes,
its priests and the country people.
They will fight against you
but shall not overcome you,
for I am with you to deliver you—
it is Yahweh who speaks."

also 1 Sam 3:1–18

PSALM 139

O Lord, you search me and you know me,
you know my resting and my rising,
you discern my purpose from afar.
You mark when I walk or lie down,
all my ways lie open to you.

Before ever a word is on my tongue
you know it, O Lord, through and through.
Behind and before you besiege me,
you hand ever laid upon me,
Too wonderful for me, this knowledge,
too high? beyond my reach.

O where can I go from your spirit,
or where can I flee from your face?
If I climb the heavens, you are there.
If I lie in the grave, you are there.

If I take the wings of the dawn
and dwell at the sea's furthest end,
even there your hand would lead me,
your right hand would hold me fast.

If I say: "Let the darkness hide me
and the light around me be night,"
even darkness is not dark for you
and the night is as clear as the day.

For it was you who created my being,
knit me together in my mother's womb.
I thank you for the wonders of my being,
for the wonders of all your creation.

Already you knew my soul,
my body held no secret from you
when I was being fashioned in secret
and molded in the depths of the earth.

Your eyes saw all my actions,
they were all of them written in your book,
every one of my days was decreed
before one of them came into being.

To me, how mysterious your thoughts,
the sum of them not to be numbered!
If I count them, they are more than the sand
to finish, I must be eternal, like you.

O search me, God, and know my heart.

O test me and know my thoughts.
See that I follow not the wrong path
and lead me in the path of life eternal.

WRITING OF FRANCIS: LORD 50–52

Almighty, eternal, just, and merciful God,
grant us in our misery (the grace)
to do for You alone
what we know You want us to do,
and always
to desire what pleases you.

Thus,
inwardly cleansed,
interiorly enlightened,
and inflamed by the fire of the Holy Spirit,
may we be able to follow
in the footprints of Your beloved Son,
our Lord Jesus Christ.

And,
by Your grace alone,
may we make our way to You,
Most High,
Who live and rule
in perfect Trinity and simple Unity,
and are glorified
God all-powerful
forever and ever.
Amen.

also 2R 10: 8–12

WRITING OF ST. CLARE: TCL 1

Among all the other gifts which we have received and continue
to receive daily from our benefactor, the Father of mercies [2 Cor
1:3], and for which we must express the deepest thanks to our glorious God, our vocation is a great gift. Since it is the more perfect and

greater, we should be so much more thankful to Him for it. For this reason the Apostle writes: "Acknowledge your calling" [1 Cor 1:26].

FRANCISCAN SOURCES: 2CEL 10

Changed now perfectly in heart, and soon to be changed in body too, he was walking one day near the church of St. Damian, which had nearly fallen to ruin and was abandoned by everyone. Led by the Spirit, he went in and fell down before the crucifix in devout and humble supplication, and smitten by unusual visitations, he found himself other than he had been when he entered. While he was thus affected, something unheard of before happened to him: the painted image of Christ crucified moved its lips and spoke. Calling him by name it said: "Francis, go, repair my house, which, as you see, is falling completely to ruin." Trembling, Francis was not a little amazed and became almost deranged by these words. He prepared himself to obey and gave himself completely to the fulfillment of this command. From then on, compassion for the crucified was rooted in his holy soul, and, as it can be piously supposedly, the stigmata of the venerable passion were deeply imprinted in his heart, though not yet upon his flesh.

VATICAN II DOCUMENT: LG 39–40

The Church, whose mystery is set forth by this sacred Council, is held, as a matter of faith, to be unfailingly holy. This is because Christ, the Son of God, who with the Father and the Spirit is hailed as "alone holy," loved the Church as His bride, giving himself up for her so as to sanctify her (cf. Eph 5:25–26); he joined her to himself as his body and endowed her with the gift of the Holy Spirit for the glory of God. Therefore, all in the Church, whether they belong to the hierarchy or are cared for by it, are called to holiness, according to the apostle's saying: "For this is the will of God, your sanctification" (1 Th 4:3; cf. Eph 1:4). This holiness of the Church is constantly shown forth in the fruits of grace which the Spirit produces in the faithful and so it must be, it is expressed in many ways by the individuals who, each in his own state of life, tend to the perfection of love, thus sanctifying others; it appears in a certain way of its own in the practice of the counsels which have been usually called "evangelical." This practice of the counsels prompted by the Holy Spirit, undertaken by many Christians whether privately or in a form or state sanctioned by the Church, gives and should give a striking witness and example of that holiness.

The Lord Jesus, divine teacher and model of all perfection, preached holiness of life (of which he is the author and maker) to each and every one of his disciples without distinction: "You, therefore, must be perfect, as your heavenly Father is perfect" (Mt 5:48). For he sent the Holy Spirit to all to move them interiorly to love God with their whole heart, with their whole soul, with their whole understanding, and with their whole strength (cf. Mk 12:30), and to love one another as Christ loved them (cf. Jn 13:34; 15:12). The followers of Christ, called by grace, and justified in the Lord Jesus, have been made sons of God in the baptism of faith and partakers of the divine nature, and so they are truly sanctified. They must therefore hold on to and perfect in their lives that sanctification which they have received from God. They are told by the apostle to live "as if fitting among saints" (Eph 5:3), and to put on "as God's chosen ones, holy and beloved: compassion, kindness, lowliness, meekness, and patience" (Col 3:12), to have the fruits of the Spirit for their sanctification (cf. Gal 5:22; Rom 6:22). But since we all offend in many ways (cf. Jas 3:2), we constantly need God's mercy and must pray everyday: "and forgive us our debts" (Mt. 6:12).

It is therefore quite clear that all Christians in any state or walk of life are called to the fullness of Christian life and to the perfection of love, and by this holiness a more human manner of life is fostered also in earthly society. In order to reach this perfection the faithful should use the strength dealt out to them by Christ's gift, so that, following in his footsteps and conformed to his image, doing the will of God in everything, they may wholeheartedly devote themselves to the glory of God and to the service of their neighbor. Thus the holiness of the People of God will grow in fruitful abundance, as is clearly shown in the history of the Church through the life of so many saints.

PAPAL STATEMENT: EN 75

The Holy Spirit is the soul of the Church. It is he who explains to the faithful the deep meaning of the teaching of Jesus and of His mystery. It is the Holy Spirit who, today just as at the beginning of the Church, acts in every evangelizer who allows himself to be possessed and led by Him. The Holy Spirit places on his lips the words which he could not find by himself, and at the same time the Holy Spirit predisposes the soul of the hearer to be open and receptive to the Good News and to the kingdom being proclaimed.

PRAYER: NINETEENTH SUNDAY IN ORDINARY TIME

Father,
we come, reborn in the Spirit,
to celebrate our sonship in the Lord Jesus Christ.
Touch our hearts,
help them grow toward the life you have promised.
Touch our lives,
make them signs of your love for all people.
Grant this through Christ our Lord. Amen.

Article 2

The Secular Franciscan Order holds a special place in this family circle. It is an organic union of all Catholic fraternities scattered throughout the world and open to every group of the faithful. In these fraternities the brothers and sisters, led by the Spirit, strive for perfect charity in their own secular state. By their profession they pledge themselves to live the gospel in the manner of Saint Francis by means of this rule approved by the Church.

THEME: THE ROLE OF THE SECULAR PERSON

GOSPEL: JN 17:9–21

> I pray for them,
> I am not praying for the world
> but for those you have given Me,
> because they belong to you:
> all I have is yours
> and all you have is mine,
> and in them I am glorified.
> I am not in the world any longer,
> but they are in the world,
> and I am coming to you.
> Holy Father,
> keep those you have given me true to your name,
> so that they may be one like us.
> While I was with them,
> I kept those you had given me true to your name.
> I have watched over them and not one is lost
> except the one who chose to be lost,
> and this was to fulfill the scriptures.
> But now I am coming to you
> and while still in the world I say these things
> to share my joy with them to the full.
> I pass your word on to them,
> and the world hated them,
> because they belong to the world
> no more then I belong to the world.

I am not asking you to remove them from the world,
but to protect them from the evil one.
They do not belong to the world
any more then I belong to the world.
Consecrate them in truth,
your word is truth.
As you sent me into the world,
I have sent them into the world,
and for their sake I consecrate myself
so that they too might be consecrated in truth.
I pray not only for these,
but for those also
who through their words will believe in me.
May they all be one.
Father, may they be one in us,
as you are in me and I am in you,
so that the world may believe it was you who sent me.

also Mt 5:13–16,48

NEW TESTAMENT: 1 JN 4:12–17

No one has ever seen God,
but as long as we love one another
God will live in us
and his love will be complete in us.
We can know that we are living in him
and he is living in us
because he lets us share his Spirit.
We ourselves saw and we testify
that the Father sent his Son
as savior of the world.
If anyone acknowledges that Jesus is the Son of God,
God lives in him, and he in God.
We ourselves have known and put our faith in
God's love toward ourselves.
God is love
and anyone who lives in love lives in God,
and God lives in him.
Love will come to its perfection in us

when we can face the day of Judgment without fear,
because even in this world
we have become as he is.

OLD TESTAMENT: DEUT 30:15–20

See, today I set before you life and prosperity, death and disaster. If you obey the commandments of Yahweh your God that I enjoin on your today, if you love Yahweh your God and follow his ways, if you keep his commandments, his laws, his customs, you will live and increase, and Yahweh your God will bless you in the land which you are entering to make your own. But if your heart strays, if you refuse to listen, if you let yourself be drawn into worshipping other gods and serving them, I tell you today, you will most certainly perish, you will not live long in the land you are crossing the Jordan to enter and possess. I call heaven and earth to witness against you today, I set before you life or death, blessing or curse. Choose life, then, so that you and your descendants may live, in the love of Yahweh your God, obeying his voice, clinging to him, for in this your life consists, and on this depends your long stay in the land which Yahweh swore to your fathers Abraham, Isaac and Jacob he would give them.

PSALM 40

I waited, I waited for the Lord
and he stooped down to me,
he heard my cry.

He drew me from the deadly pit,
from the miry clay.
He set my feet upon a rock
and made my footsteps firm.

He put a new song into my mouth:
praise of our Lord.
Many shall see and fear
and shall trust in the Lord.

Happy the man who has placed
his trust in the Lord,

and has not gone over to the rebels
who follow false gods.

How many, O Lord my God,
are the wonders and designs
that you have worked for us,
you have no equal.
Should I proclaim and speak of them:
they are more than I can tell!

In the scroll of the book it stands written
that I should do your will.
My God, I delight in your law
in the depths of my heart.

Your justice I have proclaimed
in the great assembly.
My lips I have not sealed,
you know it, O Lord.

I have not hidden your justice in my heart
but declared your faithful help.
I have not hidden your love and your truth
from the great assembly.
O Lord, you will not withhold
your compassion from me.
Your merciful love and your truth
will always guard me.

For I am beset with evils
too many to be counted.
My sins have fallen upon me
and my sight fails me.
They are more than the hairs of my head
and my heart sinks.

O Lord, come to my rescue,
Lord, come to my aid.

O let there be rejoicing and gladness
for all who seek you.
Let them ever say: "The Lord is great,"
who love your saving help.

As for me, wretched and poor,
the Lord thinks of me.
You are my rescuer, my help,
O God, do not delay.

WRITING OF FRANCIS: 1R 23:7

And all of us lesser brothers, useless servants, humbly ask and beg all those who wish to serve the Lord God within the holy, catholic, and apostolic church, and all the following order: priests, deacons, all religious men and all religious women, all lay brothers and youths, the poor and the needy, kings and princes, workers and farmers, servants and masters, all virgins and continent and married women, all lay people, men and women, all children, adolescents, the young and the old, the healthy and the sick, all the small and the great, all peoples, races, tribes, and tongues, all nations and all people everywhere on earth who are and who will be —that all of us may persevere in the true faith and in penance, for otherwise no one will be saved.

WRITING OF CLARE: BCL 8–9

On earth, may He increase His grace and virtues among His servants and handmaids of His Church Militant. In heaven, may He exalt and glorify you in His Church Triumphant among all His men and women saints.

FRANCISCAN SOURCES: 1CEL 37

Thanksgiving and voice of praise resounded everywhere so that many put aside worldly cares and gained knowledge of themselves from the life and teaching of the most blessed Francis, and they longed to attain love and reverence for their Creator. Many of the people, both noble and ignoble, cleric and lay, impelled by divine inspiration, began to come to St. Francis, wanting to carry on the battle constantly under his discipline and under his leadership. All of these the holy man of God, like a plenteous river of heavenly grace, watered with streams of gifts, he enriched the field of their hearts with flowers of virtue, for he was an excellent craftsman, and, according to his plan, rule, and teaching, proclaimed before all, the Church is being renewed in both sexes, and the threefold army of those to be served is triumphing. To all he gave a norm of life, and he showed in truth the way of salvation in every walk of life.

also 3Soc 54,60

VATICAN II DOCUMENT: LG 31

The term "laity" is here understood to mean all the faithful except those in Holy Orders and those who belong to a religious state approved by the Church. That is, the faithful who by Baptism are incorporated into Christ, are placed in the People of God, and in their own way share the priestly, prophetic, and kingly office of Christ, and to the best of their ability carry on the mission of the whole Christian people in the Church and in the world.

Their secular character is proper and peculiar to the laity. Although those in Holy Order may sometimes be engaged in secular activities, or even practice a secular profession, yet by reason of their particular vocation, they are principally and expressly ordained to the sacred ministry. At the same time, religious give outstanding and striking testimony that the world cannot be transfigured and offered to God without the spirit of the beatitudes. But by reason of their special vocation it belongs to the laity to seek the kingdom of God by engaging in temporal affairs and directing them according to God's will. They live in the world, that is, they are engaged in each and every work and business of the earth and in ordinary circumstances of social and family life which, as it were, constitute their very existence. There they are called by God that, being led by the Spirit to the Gospel, they may contribute to the sanctification of the world, as from within like leaven, by fulfilling their own particular duties. Thus, especially by the witness of their life, resplendent in faith, hope and charity they must manifest Christ to others. It pertains to them in a special way to illuminate and order all temporal things with which they are so closely associated that these may be effected and grow according to Christ and may be to the glory of the Creator and Redeemer.

also AA 5
    AG 15g, 21c
    GS 43b

PAPAL STATEMENT: EN 70

Lay people, whose particular vocation places them in the midst of the world and in charge of the most varied temporal tasks, must for this very reason exercise a very special form of evangelization.

Their primary and immediate task is not to establish and develop the ecclesial community—this is the specific role of the pastors—but to put to use every Christian and evangelical possibility latent but already present and active in the affairs of the world. Their own field of evangelizing activity is the vast and complicated world of politics, society and economics, but also the world of culture, of the sciences and the arts, of international life, of the mass media. It also includes other realities which are open to evangelization, such as human love, the family, the education of children and adolescents, professional work and suffering. The more Gospel-inspired lay people there are engaged in these realities, clearly involved in them, competent to promote them and conscious that they must exercise to the full their Christian powers which are often buried and suffocated, the more these realities will be at the service of the kingdom of God and therefore of salvation in Jesus Christ, without in any way losing or sacrificing their human content but rather pointing to a transcendent dimension which is often disregarded.

PRAYER: FOR THE LAITY

> God our Father,
> you send the power of the gospel into the world
> as a life-giving leaven.
> Fill with the Spirit of Christ
> those whom you call to live in the midst of the world
> and its concerns,
> help them by their work on earth
> to build up your eternal kingdom.
> We ask this through Christ our Lord. Amen.

Article 3

The present rule, succeeding "Memoriale Propositi" (1221), and the rules approved by the Supreme Pontiffs Nicholas IV and Leo XIII, adapts the Secular Franciscan Order to the needs and expectations of the Holy Church in the conditions of changing times. Its interpretation belongs to the Holy See and its application will be made by the General Constitutions and particular statutes.

THEME: RULE OF LIFE AS MARROW OF THE GOSPEL

GOSPEL: MK 12:28–34

One of the scribes who had listened to them debating and had observed how well Jesus had answered them, now came up and put a question to him, "Which is the first of all the commandments?" Jesus replied, "This is the first: Listen, Israel, the Lord our God is the one Lord, and you must love the Lord your God with all your heart, with all your soul, with all your mind and with all your strength. The second is this: You must love your neighbor as yourself. There is no commandment greater than these." The scribe said to him, "Well spoken, Master, what you have said is true: that he is one and there is no other. To love him with all your heart, with all your understanding and strength, and to love your neighbor as yourself, this is far more important than any holocaust or sacrifice." Jesus, seeing how wisely he had spoken, said, "You are not far from the kingdom of God." And after that no one dared to question him.

NEW TESTAMENT: GAL 2:19–20

Through the Law I am dead to the Law, so that now I can live for God. I have been crucified with Christ, and the life I live now is not with my own life but with the life of Christ who lives in me. The life I now live in this body I live in faith: faith in the Son of God who loved me and who sacrificed himself for my sake.

OLD TESTAMENT: DEUT 10:12–22

And now, Israel, what does Yahweh your God ask of you? Only this: to fear Yahweh your God, to follow all his ways, to love, to serve Yahweh your God with all your heart and all your soul, to keep the commandments and laws of Yahweh that for your good I lay down for you today.

To Yahweh your God belong indeed heaven and the heaven of heavens, the earth and all it contains, yet it was on your fathers that Yahweh set his heart for love of them, and after them of all the nations chose their descendants, you yourselves, up to the present day. Circumcise your heart then and be obstinate no longer, for Yahweh your God is God of gods and Lord of lords, the great God, triumphant and terrible, never partial, never to be bribed. It is he who sees justice done for the orphan and the widow, who loves the stranger and gives him food and clothing. Love the stranger then, for you were strangers in the land of Egypt. It is Yahweh your God you must fear and serve, you must cling to him, in his name take your oaths. He it is you must praise, he is your God, for you he has done these great and terrible things you have seen with your own eyes, and though your fathers numbered only seventy when they went down to Egypt, Yahweh your God has made you as many as the stars of heaven.

also Lv 19:1–2,37
    Deut 30:10–14

PSALM 19B

> The law of the Lord is perfect,
> it revives the soul.
> The rule of the Lord is to be trusted
> it gives wisdom to the simple.
>
> The precepts of the Lord are right,
> they gladden the heart.
> The command of the Lord is clear,
> it gives light to the eyes.
>
> The fear of the Lord is holy,
> abiding for ever.

The decrees of the Lord are truth
and all of them just.

They are more to be desired than gold,
than the purest of gold,
and sweeter are they than honey,
than honey from the comb.

So in them your servant finds instructions
great reward is in their keeping.
But who can detect all his errors?
From hidden faults acquit me.

From presumption restrain your servant
and let it not rule me.
Then shall I be blameless,
clean from grave sin.

May the spoken words of my mouth
the thoughts of my heart,
win favor in your sight, O Lord,
my rescuer, my rock!

WRITING OF FRANCIS: 2LF 86–88

In the name of the Father and of the Son and of the Holy Spirit.
Amen. I, Brother Francis, your little servant, ask and implore you in
the love which is God and with the desire to kiss your feet, to
receive these words and others of our Lord Jesus Christ with humility and love, and observe (them) and put (them) into practice. And
to all men and women who will receive them kindly (and) understand their meaning and pass them on to others by their example: If
they have persevered in them to the end, may the Father and the
Son and the Holy Spirit bless them. Amen.

also 1R 24:1–5

WRITING OF CLARE: TCL 17

In the Lord Jesus Christ, I admonish and exhort all my sisters,
both those here present and those to come, to strive always to imi-

tate the way of holy simplicity, humility, and poverty and to preserve the integrity of our holy manner of life, as we were taught by our blessed Father Francis from the beginning our conversion to Christ.

FRANCISCAN SOURCES: 2CEL 208

Francis glowed most ardently for the common profession and the rule, and he blessed with a very special blessing those who would be zealous about it. For he called the Rule the book of life, the hope of salvation, the marrow of the Gospel, the way of perfection, the key to paradise, the agreement of a perpetual covenant. He wanted it to be had by all, to be known by all, and he wanted it to speak everywhere to the interior man unto his comfort in weariness and unto a remembrance of the vows he had made. He taught them to keep it ever before their eyes as a reminder of the life they were to live, and what is more, that they should die with it.

VATICAN II DOCUMENT: PC 2,3

The up-to-date renewal of the religious life comprises both a constant return to the sources of the whole of the Christian life and to the primitive inspiration of the institutes, and their adaptation to the changed conditions of our time....

The manner of life, of prayer and of work, should be in harmony with the present-day physical and psychological condition of the members. It should also be in harmony with the needs of the apostolate, in the measure that the nature of each institute requires, with the requirements of culture and with social and economic circumstances. This should be the case everywhere, but especially in mission territories.

The mode of government of the institutes should also be examined according to the same criteria.

For this reason, constitutions, directories, books of customs, of prayer, of ceremonies and such like should be properly revised, obsolete prescriptions being suppressed, and should be brought into line with conciliar documents.

PAPAL STATEMENT: SF 2

My exhortation is this: study, love, live the Rule of the Secular Franciscan Order approved for you by my predecessor Paul VI. It is an authentic treasure in your hands, in keeping with the spirit of the Second Vatican Council and in response to all that the Church expects of you.

Love, study, and love this your Rule, because the values contained in it are eminently evangelical. Live these values in fraternity and live them in the world, in which through your same secular vocation you are involved and rooted. Live these evangelical values in your families, transmitting faith with prayer, example, education—and live the evangelical exigencies of reciprocal love, and fidelity and respect for life (SFO Rule, 17).

Above all be witnesses to the Father and of his design of love for all people and make prayer and contemplation the soul of all you are and do (SFO Rule, 8).

"The Church has need of you so that the world can be able to rediscover the primacy of spiritual values."

Let your presence bring above all, a message rich in joy, of happiness and profound faith, of harmony and of peace, and thus by your lives and your works be proclaimers of Christ and the Kingdom of God.

also EN 3
    ET 51

PRAYER: TWENTY-FIFTH SUNDAY IN ORDINARY TIME

> Father in heaven,
> the perfection of justice is found in your love
> and the human family is in need of your law.
> Help us to find this love in each other
> that justice may be attained
> through obedience to you law.
> We ask this through Christ our Lord. Amen.

chapter two

The Way of Life

T Article 4

The rule and life of the Secular Franciscans is this: to observe the gospel of our Lord Jesus Christ by following the example of Saint Francis of Assisi, who made Christ the inspiration and the center of his life with God and people.

Christ, the gift of the Father's love, is the way to him, the truth into which the Holy Spirit leads us, and the life which he has come to give abundantly.

Secular Franciscans should devote themselves especially to careful reading of the gospel, going from gospel to life and life to the gospel.

THEME: JESUS CHRIST AS CENTER AND INSPIRATION OF LIFE

GOSPEL: JN 14:6–13

Jesus said,
"I am the Way, the Truth and the Life.
No one can come to the Father except through me.
If you know me, you know my Father too.

From this moment you know him and have seen him."

Philip said, "Lord, let us see the Father and then we shall be satisfied." "Have I been with you all this time, Philip?" said Jesus to him, "and you still do not know me?

"To have seen me is to have seen the Father,
so how can you say, 'Let us see the Father?'
Do you not believe
that I am in the Father and the Father is in me?
The words I say to you I do not speak as from myself:
it is the Father, living in Me, who is doing this work.
You must believe me when I say
that I am in the Father and the Father is in me,
believe it on the evidence of this work, if for no
              other reason.
I tell you most solemnly,
whoever believes in me
will perform the same works as I do myself,
he will perform even greater works
because I am going to the Father.
Whatever you ask for in my name I will do,
so that the Father may be glorified in the Son."

also Jn 3:14–21

NEW TESTAMENT: PHIL 3:8–14

I believe nothing can happen that will outweigh the supreme advantage of knowing Christ Jesus my Lord. For him I have accepted the loss of everything, and I look on everything as so much rubbish if only I can have Christ and be given a place in him. I am no longer trying for perfection by my own efforts, the perfection that comes from the Law, but I want only the perfection that comes through faith in Christ, and is from God and based on faith. All I want is to know Christ and the power of his resurrection and to share his sufferings by reproducing the pattern of his death. Not that I have become perfect yet: I have not yet won, but I am still running, trying to capture the prize for which Christ Jesus captured me. I can assure you my brothers, I am far from thinking that

I have already won. All I can say is that I forget the past and strain ahead for what is still to come. I am racing for the finish, for the prize to which God calls us upwards to receive in Christ Jesus.

also Gal 2:19–20

OLD TESTAMENT: IS 9:1–6

The people that walked in darkness
has seen a great light;
on those who live in a land of deep shadow
a light has shown.
You have made their gladness greater,
you have made their joy increase;
they rejoice in your presence
as men rejoice at harvest time,
as men are happy when they are dividing the spoils.
For the yoke that was weighing on him,
the bar across his shoulders,
the rod of his oppressor,
these you break as on the day of Midian.
For all the footgear of battle,
every cloak rolled in blood,
is burnt,
and consumed by fire.
For there is a child born for us,
a Son given to us
and dominion is laid on his shoulders,
and this is the name they give him:
Wonder-Counselor, Mighty-God,
Eternal-Father, Prince-of-Peace.

PSALM 16

Preserve me, God, I take refuge in you.
I say to the Lord: "You are my God.
My happiness lies in you alone."

He has put into my heart a marvelous love
for the faithful ones who dwell in his land.

Those who choose other gods increase their sorrows.
Never will I offer their offerings of blood.
Never will I take their name upon my lips.

O Lord, it is you who are my portion and cup,
it is you yourself who are my prize.
The lot marked out for me is my delight:
welcome indeed the heritage that falls to me!

I will bless the Lord who gives me counsel,
who even at night directs my heart.
I keep the Lord ever in my sight:
since he is at my right hand, I shall stand firm.

And so my heart rejoices, my soul is glad,
even my body shall rest in safety.
For you will not leave my soul among the dead,
nor let your beloved know decay.

You will show me the path of life,
the fullness of joy in your presence,
at your right hand happiness for ever.

WRITING OF FRANCIS: 1R 22:25–27,41

Let us be very much on our guard so that we do not lose or turn away our mind and heart from the Lord under the guide of (achieving) some reward or (doing) some work or (providing) some help. But in the holy love which is God, I beg all (my) brothers, both the ministers and the others, as they overcome every obstacle and put aside every care and anxiety, to strive as best they can to serve, love, honor, and adore the Lord God with a clean heart and a pure mind, for this is what He desires above all things.

And let us make a home and dwelling place for Him Who is the Lord God Almighty, Father, Son, and Holy Spirit....

Let us, therefore, hold onto the words, the life, and the teachings and the Holy Gospel of Him Who humbled Himself to ask His Father for us and to make His name known to us.

WRITING OF CLARE: 2L 18–22

As a poor virgin, embrace the poor Christ. Look upon him who became contemptible for you, and follow Him, making yourself contemptible in the world for Him. Your Spouse, though more beautiful than the children of men [Ps 44:3], became, for your salvation, the lowest of men, despised, struck, scouraged untold times throughout His whole body, and then died amid the sufferings of the Cross. O most noble Queen, gaze upon Him, consider Him, contemplate Him, as you desire to imitate Him. If you suffer with Him, you shall reign with Him, if you weep with Him, you shall rejoice with Him; if you die with Him on the cross of tribulation, you shall possess heavenly mansions in the splendor of the saints and, in the Book of Life, your name shall be called glorious amng men.

FRANCISCAN SOURCES: 1CEL 84

Francis' highest intention, his chief desire, his uppermost purpose was to observe the holy Gospel in all things and through all things and, with perfect vigilance, with all zeal, with all the longing of his mind and all the fervor of his heart, "to follow the teaching and the footsteps of our Lord Jesus Christ." He would recall Christ's words through persistent meditation and bring to Him his deed through the most penetrating consideration. The humility of the Incarnation and the charity of the Passion occupied his memory particularly, to the extent that he wanted to think of hardly anything else.

VATICAN II DOCUMENT: AA 4

Christ, sent by the Father, is the source of the Church's whole apostolate. Clearly then, the fruitfulness of the apostolate of lay people depends on their living union with Christ, as the Lord said himself: "Whoever dwells in me and I in him bears much fruit, for separated from me you can do nothing" (Jn 15:5). This life of intimate union with Christ in the Church is maintained by the spiritual helps common to all the faithful, chiefly by active participation in the liturgy. Laymen should make such a use of these helps that, while meeting their human obligations in the ordinary conditions of life, they do not separate their union with Christ from their ordinary life, but through the very performance of their tasks, which are God's will for them, actually promote the growth of their union with him. This is the path along which laymen must advance, fervently, joyfully, overcoming difficulties with prudent, patient efforts. Family cares should not be foreign to the spirituality, nor any other temporal interest, in the words of the apostle: "Whatever you are doing, whether speaking or acting, do everything in the name of the Lord Jesus Christ, giving thanks to God the Father through him" (Col 3:17).

A life like this calls for a continuous exercise of faith, hope and charity.

Only the light of faith and meditation on the Word of God can enable us to find everywhere and always the God "in whom we live and exist" (Acts 17:28), only thus can we seek his will in everything, see Christ in all men, acquaintance or stranger, make sound judgments on the true meaning and value of temporal realities both in themselves and in relation to man's end.

Those with such a faith live in the hope of the revelation of the sons of God, keeping in mind the cross and resurrection of the Lord.

On life's pilgrimage they are hidden with Christ in God, are free from the slavery of riches, are in search of the goods that last forever. Generously they exert all their energies in extending God's kingdom, in making the Christian spirit a vital energizing force in the temporal sphere. In life's trials they draw courage from hope, "convinced that present sufferings are no measure of the future glory to be revealed in us" (Rom 8:18).

With the love that comes from God prompting them, they do good to all, especially to their brothers in the faith (cf. Gal 6:10), putting aside "all ill will and deceit, all hypocrisy, envy and slander" (1 Pet 2:1), in this way attracting men to Christ. Divine love, "poured into our hearts by the Holy Spirit who has been given to us" (Rom 5:5), enables lay people to express concretely in their lives the spirit of the Beatitudes. Following in Jesus' poverty, they feel no depression in want, no pride in plenty, imitating the humble Christ, they are not greedy for vain show (cf. Gal 5:26). They strive instead to please God rather than men, always ready to abandon everything for Christ (cf. Lk 14:26) and to endure persecution in the cause of right (cf. Mt 5:10), having in mind the Lord's saying: "If any man wants to come my way let him renounce self and take up his cross and follow me" (Mt 16:24). Preserving a Christian friendship with one another, they afford mutual support in all needs.

This lay spirituality will take its particular character from the circumstances of one's state in life (married and family life, celibacy, widowhood), from one's state of health and from one's professional and social activity. Whatever the circumstances, each one has received suitable talents and these should be cultivated, as should also the personal gifts he has from the Holy Spirit.

Similarly laymen who have followed their particular vocation and become members of any of the associations or institutions approved by the Church, aim sincerely at making their own the forms of spirituality proper to their bodies.

also LG 3
    AG 8

PAPAL STATEMENT: **RH 13**

The Church wishes to serve this single end: that each person may be able to find Christ, in order that Christ may walk with person the path of life, with the power of the truth about man and the world that is contained in the mystery of the Incarnation and Redemption and with the power of the love that is radiated by that truth. Against a background of the ever increasing historical processes, which seem at the present time to have results especially within the spheres of various systems, ideological concepts of the world and regimes, Jesus Christ becomes, in a way, newly present, in spite of all apparent absences, in spite of all the limitations of the presence and of the institutional activities of the Church. Jesus Christ becomes present with the power of the truth and the love that are expressed in him with unique unrepeatable fullness, in spite of the shortness of his life on earth and the ever greater shortness of his public activity.

Jesus Christ is the chief way for the Church. He himself is our way "to the Father's house" and is the way to each man. On this way leading from Christ to man, on this way on which Christ unites himself with each man, nobody can halt the Church. This is an exigency of man's temporal welfare and of his eternal welfare.

also RH 10a, 11c
    EN 27, 29

PRAYER: CHRISTMAS, MASS DURING THE DAY

> God of love, Father of all,
> the darkness that covered the earth
> has given way to the bright dawn of your Word made flesh.
> Make us people of this light.
> Make us faithful to your Word,
> that we may bring your life to the waiting world.
> Grant this through Christ our Lord. Amen.

Article 5:

Secular Franciscans, therefore, should seek to encounter the living and active person of Christ in their brothers and sisters, in Sacred Scripture, in the Church, and in liturgical activity. The faith of Saint Francis, who often said, "I see nothing bodily of the Most High Son of God in this world except his most holy body and blood," should be the inspiration and pattern of their eucharistic life.

THEME: SEEKING THE LORD JESUS THROUGHOUT LIFE

GOSPEL: JN 1:1–14

In the beginning was the Word:
the Word was with God
and the Word was God.
He was with God in the beginning.
Through him all things came to be,
not one thing had its being but through him.
All that came to be had life in him
and that life was the light of Men,
a light that shines in the dark,
a light that darkness could not overpower.
A man came, sent by God.
His name was John.
He came as a witness,
as a witness to speak for the light,
so that everyone might believe through him.
He was not the light,
only a witness to speak for the light.
The Word was the true light
that enlightens all men,
and he was coming into the world.
He was in the world
that had its being through him,
and the world did not know him.
He came to his own domain
and his own people did not accept him.
But to all who did accept him

> he gave power to become children of God,
> to all who believe in the name of him
> who was born not out of human stock
> or urge of the flesh
> or of will of man
> but of God himself.
> The Word was made flesh,
> he lived among us,
> and we saw his glory,
> the glory that is his as the only Son of the Father
> full of grace and truth.

also Mt 11:25–30
   Jn 6:44–51

NEW TESTAMENT: HEB 12:2–3

Let us not lose sight of Jesus, who leads us in our faith and brings it to perfection: for the sake of the joy which was still in the future he endured the cross, disregarding the shamefulness of it, and from now on has taken his place at the right of God's throne. Think of the way he stood such opposition from sinners and then you will not give up for want of courage.

OLD TESTAMENT: JER 29:12–14

When you call to me, and come to plead with me, I will listen to you. When you seek me you shall find me, when you seek me with all your heart, I will let you find me—it is Yahweh who speaks. I will restore your fortunes and gather you from all the nations and all the place where I have dispersed you—it is Yahweh who speaks. I will bring you back to the place from which I exiled you.

also 2 Chron 15:2–4
   1 Kgs 19:4–13

PSALM 27

> The Lord is my light and my help,
> whom shall I fear?

The Lord is the stronghold of my life,
before whom shall I shrink?

When evil-doers draw near
to devour my flesh,
it is they, my enemies and foes,
who stumble and fall.

Though an army encamp against me
my heart would not fear.
Though war break out against me
even then would I trust.

There is one thing I ask of the Lord
for this I long,
to live in the house of the Lord,
all the days of my life,
to savor the sweetness of the Lord,
to behold his temple.

For there he keeps me safe in his tent
in the day of evil.
He hides me in the shelter of his tent
on a rock he sets me safe.

O Lord, hear my voice when I call,
have mercy and answer.
Of you my heart has spoken:
"Seek his face."

It is your face, O Lord, that I seek,
hide not your face.
Dismiss not your servant in anger,
you have been my help.

Do not abandon or forsake me,
O God my help!
Though father and mother forsake me
the Lord will receive me.

Instruct me, Lord, in your way,
on an even path lead me.
When they lie in ambush protect me

from my enemy's greed.
False witnesses rise against me,
breathing out fury.

I am sure I shall see the Lord's goodness
in the land of the living.
Hope in him, hold firm and take heart.
Hope in the Lord!

WRITING OF FRANCIS: ADM 1,16–23

See, daily He humbles Himself as when He came from the royal throne into the womb of the Virgin; daily He comes to us in a humble form; daily he comes down from the bosom of the Father upon the altar in the hands of the priest. And as he appeared to the holy apostles in true flesh, so now he reveals Himself to us in the sacred bread. And as they saw only His flesh by means of their bodily sight, yet believed Him to be God as they contemplated Him with the eyes of faith, so, as we see bread and wine with (our) bodily eyes, we too are to see and firmly believe them to be His most holy Body and Blood living and true. And in this way the Lord is always with his faithful, as He Himself says: "Behold I am with you even to the end of the world."

also PrCruc

WRITING OF CLARE: 4L 9–13

Happy, indeed, is she to whom it is given to share this sacred
    banquet, to cling with all her heart to [Jesus]
Whose beauty all the heavenly hosts admire unceasingly,
Whose love inflames our love,
Whose contemplation is our refreshment,
Whose graciousness is our joy,
Whose gentleness fills us to overflowing,
Whose remembrance brings a gentle light,
Whose fragrance will revive the dead,
Whose glorious visition will be the happiness of all
    the citizens of the heavenly Jerusalem.

FRANCISCAN SOURCES: 1CEL 115

The brothers, moreover, who lived with him knew how his daily and continuous talk was of Jesus and how sweet and tender his conversation was, how kind and filled with love his talk with them. His mouth spoke out of the abundance of his heart, and the fountain of enlightened love that filled his whole being bubbled forth outwardly. Indeed, he was always occupied with Jesus; Jesus he bore in his heart, Jesus in his mouth, Jesus in his ears, Jesus in his eyes, Jesus in his hands, Jesus in the rest of his members. O how often, when he sat down to eat, hearing or speaking or thinking of Jesus, he forgot bodily food, as we read of the holy one: "Seeing, he did not see, and hearing he did not hear." Indeed, many times, as he went along the way meditating on and singing of Jesus, he would forget his journey and invite all the elements to praise Jesus. And because he ways bore and preserved Christ Jesus and him crucified in his heart with a wonderful love, he was marked in a most glorious way above all others with the seal of him whom in a rapture of mind he contemplated sitting in inexpressible and incomprehensible glory at the right hand of the Father, with whom he, the co-equal and most high Son of the Most High, lives and reigns, conquers and governs in union with the Holy Spirit, God eternally glorious through all ages forever. Amen.

VATICAN II DOCUMENT: GS 45

The Word of God, through whom all things were made, was made flesh, so that as perfect man he could save all men and sum up all things in himself. The Lord is the goal of human history, the focal point of the desires of history and civilization, the center of mankind, the joy of all hearts, and the fulfillment of all aspirations. it is he whom the Father raised from the dead, exalted and placed at his right hand, constituting him judge of the living and the dead. Animated and drawn together in his Spirit we press onward on our journey toward the consummation of history which fully corresponds to the plan of his love: "to unite all things in him, things in heaven and things on earth" (Eph 1:10).

The Lord himself said: "Behold, I am coming soon, bringing my recompense, to repay every one for what he has done. I am the alpha and the omega, the first and the last, the beginning and the end" (Apoc 22:12–13).

PAPAL STATEMENT: RH 7C

Through the Church's consciousness, which the Council considerably developed, through all levels of this self-awareness, and through all the fields of activity in which the Church expresses, finds and confirms herself, we must constantly aim at him "who is the head," "through whom are all things and through whom we exist," who is both "the way, and the truth" and "the resurrection and the life," seeing whom we see the Father, and who had to go away from us—that is, by his death on the Cross and then by his Ascension into heaven—in order that the Counselor should come to us and should keep coming to us as the Spirit of truth. In him are "all the treasures of wisdom and knowledge," and the Church is his Body. "By her relationship with Christ, the Church is a kind of sacrament or sign and means of intimate union with God, and of the unity of all mankind," and the source of this is he, he himself, he the Redeemer.

also ET 33
    ES 36

PRAYER: TWENTY-FIRST SUNDAY IN ORDINARY TIME

Lord our God,
all truth is from you,
and you alone bring oneness of heart.
Give your people the joy
of hearing your word in every sound
and of longing for your presence more than for life itself.
May all the attractions of a changing world
serve only to bring us
the peace of your kingdom
which this world does not give.
Grant this through Christ our Lord. Amen.

Article 6

They have been made living members of the Church by being buried and raised with Christ in baptism, they have been united more intimately with the Church by profession. Therefore, they should go forth as witnesses and instruments of her mission among all people, proclaiming Christ by their life and words.

Called like Saint Francis to rebuild the Church and inspired by his example, let them devote themselves energetically to living in full communion with the pope, bishops, and priests, fostering an open and trusting dialogue of apostolic effectiveness and creativity.

THEME: SHARERS AND WITNESSES OF CHRIST'S MISSION

GOSPEL: MK 16:15–20

Jesus said, "Go out to the whole world, proclaim the Good News to all creation. He who believes and is baptized will be saved, he who does not believe will be condemned. These are the signs that will be associated with believers: in my name they will cast out devils, they will have the gift of tongues, they will pick up snakes in their hands, and be unharmed if they drink deadly poison, they will lay their hands on the sick, who will recover."

And so the Lord Jesus, after he had spoken to them, was taken up into heaven: there at the right hand of God he took his place, while they, going out, preached everywhere, the Lord working with them and confirming the word by the signs that accompanied it.

also Jn 15:4–8

NEW TESTAMENT: 2 COR 5:14–20

The love of Christ overwhelms us when we reflect that if one man has died for all, then all men should be dead, and the reason he died for all was so that living men should live no longer for themselves, but for him who died and was raised to life for them.

From now onwards, therefore, we do not judge anyone by the standards of the flesh. Even if we did once know Christ in the flesh that is not how we know him now. And for anyone who is in Christ there is a new creation; the old creation has gone, and now a new one is here. It is all God's work. It was God who reconciled us to himself through Christ and gave us the work of handing on this reconciliation. In other words, God in Christ was reconciling the world to himself, not holding men's faults against them, and he has entrusted to us the news that they are reconciled. So we are ambassadors for Christ, it is as though God were appealing through us, and the appeal that we make in Christ's name is: be reconciled to God.

also Acts 10:37–43
    Eph 3:2–12

OLD TESTAMENT: IS 43:8–12

Bring forward the people that are blind, yet have eyes,
that are deaf and yet have ears.
Let all the nations muster
and assemble with every race.
Which of them ever declared this
or foretold this in the past?
Let them bring their witnesses to prove them right,
let men hear them so that they may say, "It is true."
You yourselves are my witnesses—it is Yahweh who
        speaks—
my servants whom I have chosen,
that men may know and believe me
and understand that it is I.
No god was formed before me,
nor will be after me.
I, I am Yahweh,
there is no other savior but me.
It is I who have spoken, have saved, have made the
        proclamations:
not any stranger among you.
You are my witnesses—it is Yahweh who speaks—
and I, I am your God, I am he from eternity.

PSALM 145

I will give you glory, O God my King,
I will bless your name for ever.
I will bless you day after day
and praise your name for ever.
The Lord is great, highly to be praised,
his greatness cannot be measured.

Age to age shall proclaim your works,
shall declare your mighty deeds,
shall speak of your splendor and glory,
tell the tale of your wonderful works.

They will speak of your terrible deeds,
recount your greatness and might.
They will recall your abundant goodness,
age to age shall ring out your justice.

The Lord is kind and full of compassion
slow to anger, abounding in love.
How good is the Lord to all,
compassionate to all his creatures.

All your creatures shall thank you, O Lord,
and your friends shall repeat their blessing.
They shall speak of the glory of your reign
and declare your might, O God,

to make known to men your mighty deeds
and the glorious splendor of your reign.
Yours is an everlasting kingdom,
your rule lasts from age to age.

The Lord is faithful in all his words
and loving in all his deeds.
The Lord supports all who fall
and raises all who are bowed down.

The eyes of all creatures look to you
and you give them their food in due time.
You open wide your hand,
grant the desire of all who live.

The Lord is just in all his ways
and loving in all his deeds.
He is close to all who call him,
who call on him from their hearts.

He grants the desires of those who fear him,
he hears their cry and he saves them.
The Lord protects all who love him,
but the wicked he will utterly destroy.
Let me speak the praise of the Lord,
let all mankind bless his holy name
for ever, for ages unending.

WRITING OF FRANCIS: TestS 1–5

I bless all my brothers, (those) who are in the Order, and (those) who will come until the end of the world. Since because of my weakness and the pain of my sickness I am not strong enough to speak, I make known my will to my brothers briefly in these three phrases, namely: as a sign that they remember my blessing and my testament, let them always love one another, let they always love and be faithful to our Lady Holy Poverty, and let them always be faithful and subject to the prelates and all clerics of Holy Mother Church.

also SP 87

WRITING OF CLARE: TCl 13

I commend all my sisters... to our holy Mother the Church of Rome.... [May] his little flock observe that which our Lord and Father has begotten in his holy Church by word and example of our blessed Father Francis.

also RCl 1:3

FRANCISCAN SOURCES: 1CEL 62

Francis thought that the faith of the holy Roman Church was by all means to be preserved, honored, and imitated, that faith in which alone is found the salvation of all who are to be saved. He revered priests and he had a great affection for every ecclesiastical order.

also 2Cel 24

VATICAN II DOCUMENT: LG 33

Gathered together in the People of God and established in the one Body of Christ under one head, the laity—no matter who they are—have, as living members, the vocation of applying to the building up of the Church and to its continual sanctification all the powers which they have received from the goodness of the Creator and from the grace of the Redeemer.

The apostolate of the laity is a sharing in the salvific mission of the Church. Through Baptism and Confirmation, all are appointed to this apostolate by the Lord himself. Moreover, by the sacraments, and especially by the Eucharist, that love of God and man which is the soul of the apostolate is communicated and nourished. The laity, however, are given this special vocation: to make the Church present and fruitful in those places and circumstances where it is only through them that she can become the salt of the earth. Thus, every lay person, through those gifts given to him, is at once the witness and the living instrument of the mission of the Church itself "according to the measure of Christ's bestowal" (Eph 4:7).

Besides this apostolate which belongs to absolutely every Christian, the laity can be called in different ways to more and immediate cooperation in the apostolate of the hierarchy, like those men and women who helped the apostle Paul in the Gospel, laboring much in the Lord (cf. Phil 4:3; Rom 16:3ff). They have, moreover, the capacity of being appointed by the hierarchy to some ecclesiastical offices with a view to a spiritual end.

All the laity, then, have the exalted duty of working for the ever greater spread of the divine plan of salvation to all men, of every epoch and all over the earth. Therefore may the way be clear for them to share diligently in the salvific work of the church according to their ability and the needs of the times.

also AA 6
    AG 5, 35

PAPAL STATEMENT: RH 11E

Jesus Christ is the stable principle and fixed center of the mission that God himself has entrusted to man. We must all share in this mission and concentrate all our forces on it, since it is more necessary than ever for modern mankind. If this mission seems to encounter greater opposition nowadays than ever before, it shows that today it is more necessary than ever before and, in spite of the opposition, more awaited than ever. Here we touch indirectly on the mystery of the divine "economy" which linked salvation and grace with the cross. It was not without reason Christ said that "the kingdom of heaven has suffered violence, and men of violence take it by force" and moreover that "the children of this world are more astute... than are the children of light." We gladly accept this rebuke, that we may be like those "violent people of God" that we have so often seen in this history of the Church and still see today, and that we may consciously join in the great mission of revealing Christ to the world, helping each person to find himself in Christ, and helping the contemporary generations of our brothers and sisters, the peoples, nations, states, mankind, developing countries and countries of opulence—in short, helping everyone to get to know "the unsearchable riches of Christ," since these riches are for every individual and are everybody's property.

also RH 10c
    EN 14,41
    ES 64

PRAYER: EIGHTH SUNDAY IN ORDINARY TIME

Father in heaven,
form us in the likeness of your Son
and deepen his life within us.
Send us as witnesses of gospel joy
into a world of fragile peace and broken promises.
Touch the hearts of all people with your love
that they in turn may love one another.
We ask this through Christ our Lord. Amen.

Article 7

United by their vocation as "brothers and sisters of penance," and motivated by the dynamic power of the gospel, let them conform their thoughts and deeds to those of Christ by means of that radical interior change which the gospel itself calls "conversion." Human frailty makes it necessary that this conversion be carried out daily. On this road to renewal the sacrament of reconciliation is the privileged sign of the Father's mercy and the source of grace.

THEME: ONGOING CHANGE OF HEART

GOSPEL: MK 1:14–15

After John had been arrested, Jesus went into Galilee. There he proclaimed the Goods News from God. "The time has come," he said, "and the kingdom of God is close at hand. Repent, and believe the Good News."

also Mt 16:24–27
    Mk 8:34–35
    Lk 9:23–26

NEW TESTAMENT: EPH 4:17–24

I want to urge you in the name of the Lord, not to go on living the aimless kind of life that pagans live. Intellectually they are in the dark, and they are estranged from the life of God, without knowledge because they have shut their hearts to it. Their sense of right and wrong once dulled, they have abandoned themselves to sexuality and eagerly pursue a career of indecency of every kind. Now that is hardly the way you have learnt from Christ, unless you failed to hear him properly when you were taught what the truth is in Jesus. You must give up your old way of life, you must put aside your old self, which gets corrupted by following illusory desires. Your mind must be renewed by a spiritual revolution so that you can put on the new self that has been created in God's way, in the goodness and holiness of truth.

also Rom 6:3–11

OLD TESTAMENT: IS 55:6–9

> Seek Yahweh while is he still to be found,
> call to him while he is still near.
> Let the wicked man abandon his way,
> the evil man his thoughts.
> Let him turn back to Yahweh who will take pity on him
> to our God who is rich in forgiving,
> for my thoughts are not your thoughts,
> my ways are not your ways—it is Yahweh who speaks.
> Yes, the heavens are as high above earth
> as my ways are above your ways,
> my thoughts above your thoughts.

also Ez 18:21–32
    Hos 14:2–10
    Joel 2:12–17
    Sir 17:17–22

PSALM 51

> Have mercy on me, God, in your kindness.
> In your compassion blot out my offense.
> O wash me more and more from my guilt
> and cleanse me from my sin.
>
> My offenses truly I know them,
> my sin is always before me.
> Against you, you alone, have I sinned,
> what is evil in your sight I have done.
>
> That you may be justified when you given sentence
> and be without reproach when you judge.
> O see, in guilt I was born,
> a sinner was I conceived.
>
> Indeed you love truth in the heart,
> then in the secret of my heart teach me wisdom.
> O purify me, then I shall be clean,
> O wash me! I shall be whiter than snow.

Make me hear rejoicing and gladness,
that the bones you have crushed may revive.
From my sins turn away your face
and blot out all my guilt.

A pure heart create for me, O God,
put a steadfast spirit within me.
Do not cast me away from your presence,
nor deprive me of your holy spirit.

Give me again the joy of your help,
and my tongue shall ring out your goodness.
O Lord, open my lips
and my mouth shall declare your praise.

For in sacrifice you take no delight,
burnt offering from me you would refuse,
my sacrifice, a contrite spirit.
A humbled, contrite heart you will not spurn.

In your goodness, show favor to Zion:
rebuild the walls of Jerusalem.
Then you will be pleased with lawful sacrifice,
holocausts offered on your altar.

WRITING OF FRANCIS: 1R 21:2-9

Fear and honor, praise and bless, give thanks and adore
the Lord God Almighty in Trinity and in Unity,
the Father and the Son and the Holy Spirit
the Creator of all.

Do penance, performing worthy fruits of penance
since we will soon die.

Give and it shall be given to you.
Forgive and you shall be forgiven.

And if you do not forgive men their sins,
the Lord will not forgive you your sins.
Confess all your sins.

Blessed are those who die in penance, for they shall be in

the kingdom of heaven.

Woe to those who do not die in penance, for they shall be
the children of the devil
whose works they do,

and they shall go into the eternal fire.
Beware and abstain from every evil and persevere in good
till the end.

also Test 1–3
    1R 23:7–8

WRITING OF CLARE: 3L 7

I see that... you have taken hold of that incomparable treasure
hidden in the field of the world and in the hearts of men (cf. Mt
13:44), within which you have purchased that field of him by whom
all things have been made from nothing.

FRANCISCAN SOURCES: 1CEL 22–23

When on a certain day the Gospel was read in that church, how
the Lord sent his disciples out to preach, the holy man of God,
assisting there, understood somewhat the words of the Gospel; after
Mass he humbly asked the priest to explain the Gospel to him more
fully. When he had set forth for him in order all these things, the
holy Francis, hearing that the disciples of Christ should not possess
gold or silver or money, not carry along the way scrip, or wallet, or
bread, or a staff, that they should not have shoes, or two tunics, but
that they should preach the kingdom of God and penance, immediately cried out exultingly: "This is what I wish, this is what I seek,
this is what I long to do with all my heart." Then the holy father,
overflowing with joy, hastened to fulfill that salutary word he had
heard. He immediately put off his shoes from his feet, put aside the
staff from his hands, was content with one tunic, and exchanged his
leather girdle for a small cord. He designed for himself a tunic that
bore a likeness to the cross, that by means of it he might beat off all
temptations of the devil, he designed a very rough tunic so that by
it he might crucify the flesh with all its vices and sins, he designed a

very poor and mean tunic, one that would not excite the covetousness of the world. The other things that he had heard, however, he longed with great diligence and the greatest reverence to perform. For he was not a deaf hearer of the Gospel, but committing all that he had heard to praiseworthy memory, he tried diligently to carry it out to the letter.

From then on he began to preach penance to all with great fervor of spirit and joy of mind, edifying his hearers with his simple words and his greatness of heart.

VATICAN II DOCUMENT: LG 8

Christ, "holy, innocent and undefiled" (Heb 7:26) knew nothing of sin (2 Cor 5:21), but came only to expiate the sins of the people (cf. Heb 2:17). The Church, however, clasping sinners to her bosom, at once holy and always in need of purification, follows constantly the path of penance and renewal.

The Church, "like a stranger in a foreign land, presses forward amid the persecutions of the world and the consolations of God," announcing the cross and death of the Lord until he comes (cf. 1 Cor 11:26). But by the power of the risen Lord she is given strength to overcome, in patience and in love, her sorrows and her difficulties, both those that are from within and those that are from without, so that she may reveal in the world, faithfully, however darkly, the mystery of her Lord until, in the consummation, it shall be manifested in full light.

PAPAL STATEMENT: EN 10

This kingdom and this salvation, which are the key words of Jesus Christ's evangelization are available to every human being as grace and mercy, and yet at the same time each individual must gain them by force—they belong to the violent, says the Lord, through toil and suffering, through a life lived according to the Gospel, through abnegation and the cross, through the spirit of the Beatitudes. But above all each individual gains them through a total interior renewal which the Gospel calls "metanoia," it is a radical conversion, a profound change of mind and heart.

also ET 11, 31, 37

PRAYER: SECOND SUNDAY OF LENT

Father of Light,
in you is found no shadow of change
but only the fullness of life and limitless truth.
Open our hearts to the voice of your Word
and free us from the original darkness that
        shadows our vision.
Restore our sight that we may look upon your Son
who calls us to repentance and a change of heart,
for he lives and reigns with you for ever and ever. Amen.

Article 8

As Jesus was the true worshipper of the Father, so let prayer and contemplation be the soul of all they are and do.

Let them participate in the sacramental life of the Church, above all the Eucharist. Let them join in liturgical prayer in one of the forms proposed by the Church, reliving the mysteries of the life of Christ.

THEME: TRUE WORSHIPPERS OF THE LORD

GOSPEL: JN 4:23–24

> But the hour will come—in fact it is already here—
> when true worshippers will worship the Father in spirit
>   and truth:
> that is the kind of worshippers
> the Father wants.
> God is spirit,
> and those who worship
> must worship in spirit and truth.

NEW TESTAMENT: 1 COR 11:23–26

This is what I received from the Lord, and in turn passed on to you: that on the same night that he was betrayed, the Lord Jesus took some bread and thanked God for it and broke it, and he said, "This is my body, which is for you: do this as a memorial of me." In the same way he took the cup after supper, and said, "This is the new covenant in my blood. Whenever you drink it, do this as a memorial of me." Until the Lord comes, therefore, every time you eat this bread and drink this cup, you are proclaiming his death.

also Eph 6:18–20
    Col 4:2–4
    1 Thes 5:16–18

OLD TESTAMENT: DAN 3:26, 39–41, 52–54, 89–90

All honor and blessing to you, Lord, God of our ancestors,
may your name be held glorious forever....
May the contrite soul, the humbled spirit be
       acceptable to you
as holocausts of rams and bullocks,
as thousands of fat lambs:
such let our sacrifice be to you today,
and may it be your will that we follow you wholeheartedly,
since those who put their trust in you will not
       be disappointed.
And now we put our whole heart into following you,
into fearing you and seeking your face once more.
May you be blessed, Lord, God of our ancestors,
be praised and extolled for ever.
Blessed be your glorious and holy name,
praised and extolled for ever.
May you be blessed in the Temple of your sacred glory,
exalted and glorified above all else for ever:
blessed on the throne of your kingdom,
praised and exalted above all else for ever....
Give thanks to the Lord, for he is good,
for his love is everlasting.
All you who worship him, bless the God of Gods,
praise him and give him thanks,
for his love is everlasting.

PSALM 111

I will thank the Lord with all my heart
in the meeting of the just and their assembly.
Great are the works of the Lord,
to be pondered by all who love them.
Majestic and glorious his work,
his justice stands firm for ever.
He makes us remember his wonders.
The Lord is compassion and love.
He gives food to those who fear him,

keeps his covenant ever in mind.
He has shown his might to his people
by giving them the lands of the nations.
His works are justice and truth:
his precepts are all of them sure,
standing firm for ever and ever:
they are made in uprightness and truth.
He has sent deliverance to his people
and established his covenant for ever
Holy his name, to be feared.
To fear the Lord is the beginning of wisdom,
all who do so prove themselves wise.
His praise shall last for ever!

WRITING OF FRANCIS: 2LF 19–24

Let us love God, therefore, and adore Him with a pure heart and a pure mind because He Who seeks this above all else has said: "The true worshipers will adore the Father in spirit and in truth." For all those who worship Him are to worship Him in the spirit of truth. And let us praise Him and pray to Him day and night saying: "Our Father Who art in heaven," since we should pray always and never lose heart.

We must also confess all our sins to a priest and receive from him the Body and Blood of our Lord Jesus Christ. He who does not eat His Flesh and does not drink His Blood cannot enter the Kingdom of God. Yet let him eat and drink worthily, since he who receives unworthily eats and drinks judgment to himself, not recognizing—that is, not discerning—the Body of the Lord.

WRITING OF CLARE: 3L 12–14

Place your mind before the mirror of eternity!
Place your soul in the brilliance of glory! (Heb 1:3)
Place your heart in the figure of the divine substance!
And transform your entire being into the image of the
Godhead Itself through contemplation.
So that you too may feel what His friends feel
     as they taste the hidden sweetness (Ps 30:20)

which God Himself has reserved
from the beginning
for those who love Him.

FRANCISCAN SOURCES: LM 10:1

Saint Francis realized that he was an exile from the Lord's presence as long as he was at home in the body, and his love of Christ had left him with no desire for the things of this earth. Therefore, he tried to keep his spirit always in the presence of God, by praying to him without intermission, so that he might not be without some comfort from his Beloved. Prayer was his chief comfort in this life of contemplation in which he became a fellow-citizen of the angels, as he penetrated the dwelling places of heaven in his eager search for his Beloved, from whom he was separated only by a partition of flesh. Prayer was his sure refuge in everything he did; he never relied on his own efforts, but put his trust in God's loving providence and cast the burden of his cares on him in insistent prayer. He was convinced that the grace of prayer was something a religious should long for above all else. No one, he declared, could make progress in God's service without it, and he used every means he could to make the friars concentrate on it. Whether he was walking or resting, he was so fervently devoted to prayer that he seemed to have dedicated to it not only his heart and his soul, but all his efforts and all his time.

also 2Cel 94–96

VATICAN II DOCUMENT: SC 2

It is the liturgy through which, especially in the divine sacrifice of the Eucharist, "the work of our redemption is accomplished," and it is through the liturgy, especially, that the faithful are enabled to express in their lives and manifest to others the mystery of Christ and the real nature of the true Church. The Church is essentially both human and divine, visible but endowed with invisible realities, zealous in action and dedicated to contemplation, present in the world, but as a pilgrim, so constituted that in her the human is directed toward and subordinated to the divine, the visible to the invisible, action to contemplation, and this present world to that city yet to come, the object of our quest. The liturgy daily builds up those who are in the Church, making of them a holy temple of the Lord, a dwelling place for God in the Spirit, to the mature measure of the fullness of Christ. At the same time it marvelously increases their power to preach Christ and thus show forth the Church, a sign lifted up among the nations, to those who are outside, a sign under which the scattered children of God may be gathered together until there is one fold and one shepherd.

also LG 50
    SC 83–84
    AA 10

PAPAL STATEMENT: RH 7

The Church never ceases to relive his death on the Cross and Resurrection, which constitute the content of the Church's daily life. Indeed, it is by the command of Christ himself, her Master, that the Church unceasingly celebrates the Eucharist, finding in it the "fountain of life and holiness," the efficacious sign of grace and reconciliation with God, and the pledge of eternal life. The Church lives his mystery, drawn unswervingly from it and continually seeks ways of bringing this mystery of her Master and Lord to humanity—to the peoples, the nations, the succeeding generations, and every individual human being—as if she were ever repeating, as the Apostle did: "For I decided to know nothing among you except Jesus Christ and him crucified." The Church stays within the sphere of the mystery of the Redemption, which has become the fundamental principle of her life and mission.

also RH 20
    ET 43, 47–48

PRAYER: VOTIVE MASS OF THE EUCHARIST

Father,
you have brought to fulfillment the work of redemption
through the Easter mystery of Christ your Son.

May we who faithfully proclaim his death and resurrection
    in these sacramental signs
experience the constant growth of your salvation in
    our lives.
We ask this through Christ our Lord. Amen.

Article 9

The Virgin Mary, humble servant of the Lord, was open to his every word and call. She was embraced and declared the protectress and advocate of his family. The Secular Franciscans should express their ardent love for her by imitating her complete self-giving and by praying earnestly and confidently.

THEME: MARY AS MOTHER AND MODEL

GOSPEL: LK 1:46–55

> Mary said,
> "My soul proclaims the greatness of the Lord
> and my spirit exults in God my savior,
> because he has looked upon his lowly handmaid.
> Yes, from this day forward all generation will call me
> blessed,
> for the Almighty has done great things for me.
> Holy is his name,
> and his mercy reaches from age to age for those
> who fear him.
> He has shown the power of his arm,
> he has routed the proud of heart.
> He has pulled down princes from their thrones and
> exalted the lowly.
> The hungry he has filled with good things,
> the rich sent empty away.
> He has come to the help of Israel his servant,
> mindful of his mercy
> —according to the promise he made to our ancestors—
> of his mercy to Abraham and to his descendants for ever."

also Lk 11:27–28
    Jn 19:25–27

NEW TESTAMENT: ROM 8:28–30

We know that by turning everything to their good, God co-

operates with all those who love him, with all those that he has
called according to his purpose. They are the ones he chose specially
long ago and intended to become true images of his Son, so that his
Son might be the eldest of many brothers. He called those he
intended for this: those he called he justified, and with those he justified he shared his glory.

also Gal 4:4–7
       Rev 12:1–6

OLD TESTAMENT: ZEC 2:14–17

> Sing, rejoice,
> daughter of Zion,
> for I am coming
> to dwell in the middle of you
> —it is Yahweh who speaks.
> Many nations will join Yahweh,
> on that day,
> they will become his people.
> (But he will remain among you,
> and you will know that Yahweh Sabbath
>   has sent me to you.)
> But Yahweh will hold Judah
> as his portion in the Holy Land,
> and again make Jerusalem his very own.
> Let all mankind be silent before Yahweh!
> For he is awakening and is coming from his holy dwelling.

also Jdt 13:18–20

PSALM 45

> My heart overflows with noble words.
> To the king I must speak the song I have made,
> my tongue as nimble as the pen of a scribe.
>
> You are the fairest of the children of men
> and graciousness is poured upon your lips:
> because God has blessed you for evermore.

O mighty one, gird your sword upon your thigh,
in splendor and state, ride on in triumph
for the cause of truth and goodness and right.

Take aim with your bow in your dread right hand.
Your arrows are sharp: peoples fall beneath you.
The foes of the king fall down and lose heart.

Your throne, O God, shall endure for ever.
A scepter of justice is the scepter of your kingdom.
Your love is for justice, your hatred for evil.

Therefore God, your God, has anointed you
with the oil of gladness above other kings:
your robes are fragrant with aloes and myrrh.

From the ivory palace you are greeted with music.
The daughters of kings are among your loved ones.
On your right stands the queen in gold of Ophir.

Listen, O daughter, give ear to my words,
forget your own people and your father's house
So will the king desire your beauty:
he is your lord, pay homage to him.
And the people of Tyre shall come with gifts,
the richest of the people shall seek your favor.
The daughter of the king is clothed with splendor,
her robes embroidered with pearls set in gold.

She is led to the king with her maiden companions
They are escorted amid gladness and joy,
they pass within the palace of the king.

Sons shall be yours in place of your fathers:
you will make them princes over all the earth.
May this song make your name for ever remembered.
May the peoples praise you from age to age.

WRITING OF FRANCIS: SALBVM 1–8

Hail, O Lady,
holy Queen,

Mary, holy Mother of God:
you are the virgin made church
and the one chosen by the most holy Father in heaven
whom he consecrated
with His most holy beloved Son
and with the Holy Spirit the Paraclete,
in whom there was and is
all the fullness of grace and every good.
Hail, His Palace!
Hail, His Tabernacle!
Hail, His Home!
Hail, His Robe!
Hail, His Servant!
Hail, His Mother!
And, (hail) all you holy virtues
which through the grace and light of the Holy Spirit
are poured into the hearts of the faithful
so that from their faithless state
you may make them faithful to God.

also OP, Antiphon

WRITING OF CLARE: 3L 18–19,24–26

Cling to His most sweet Mother who carried a Son Whom the heavens could not contain; and yet she carried Him in the little enclosure of her holy womb and held Him on her virginal lap.... Therefore, as the glorious Virgin of virgins carried Christ materially in her body, you, too, by following in His footprints (cf. 1 Pet 2:21), especially those of poverty and humility, can, without any doubt, always carry Him spiritually in your chaste and virginal body. And you will hold Him by whom you you and all things are held together (cf Wis. 1:7; Col 1:17), thus possessing that which, in comparison with the other transitory possessions of this world, you will possess more securely.

FRANCISCAN SOURCES: 2CEL 198

Toward the Mother of Jesus he was filled with an inexpressible love, because it was she who made the Lord of Majesty our brother.

He sent special praises to her, poured out prayers to her, offered her his affections, so many and so great that the tongue of man cannot recount them. But what delights us most, he made her the advocate of the order and placed under her wings the sons he was about to leave that she might cherish them and protect them to the end. Hail, advocate of the poor! Fulfill toward us your office of protectress until the time set by the Father.

also 2Cel 83, 200
    LM 2:8
    3Soc 15

VATICAN II DOCUMENT: LG 63

By reason of the gift and role of her divine motherhood, by which she is united with her Son, the Redeemer, and with her unique graces and functions, the Blessed Virgin is also intimately united to the Church. As St. Ambrose taught, the Mother of God is a type of the Church in the order of faith, charity, and perfect union with Christ. For in the mystery of the Church, which is itself right hailed mother and virgin, the Blessed Virgin stands out in eminent and singular fashion as exemplar both of virgin and mother. Through her faith and obedience she gave birth on earth to the very Son of the Father, not through the knowledge of man but by the overshadowing of the Holy Spirit, in the manner of a new Eve who placed her faith, not in the serpent of old but in God's messenger without wavering in doubt. The Son whom she brought forth is he whom God placed as the first born among many brethren (Rom 8:29), that is, the faithful, in whose generation and formation she cooperates with a mother's love.

also LG 52–53, 56
    AA 4j

PAPAL STATEMENT: MX, 4–5

Among all the titles given to the Virgin through the centuries for her motherly love for Christians, there is one that stands out: "virgo fidelis" (faithful virgin). But what does this fidelity of Mary mean? What are the dimensions of this fidelity?

The first dimension is searching. Mary was faithful when she searched for the profound meaning of the will of God in her life. Quomodo fiat? (How might this be?) she asked the angel of the Annunciation. In the Old Testament this searching is already translated into an expression of rare beauty, of profound spiritual meaning: to seek the face of the Lord. There can be no fidelity if there is not this deep-seated searching, if we cannot find in heart of man the question to which only God is the answer.

The second dimension of this fidelity is called acceptance, to accept. The "quomodo fiat" is transformed on the lips of Mary as a "fiat" (let it be). Let it be, I am willing, I accept. This is the moment of truth for fidelity, the moment in which man comes to realize that he can never fully understand the why, that there are in God's design more areas of mystery than explanations, that no matter how hard he tries, he will never be able to accept everything.

Then the person is ready to accept this mystery and give a place in his heart, as Mary kept all these things in her heart (Lk 2:19, cf. Lk 3:15). It is the moment in which man opens himself to this mystery, not in the way someone gives up facing an enigma or the absurd, but rather with the openness of someone letting himself be possessed by something—someone—bigger than his heart. This acceptance is fulfilled through faith which is the union of our being with the mystery that is revealed.

Coherence is the third dimension of fidelity. To live in accordance with what one believes. To adjust one's life to what one adheres to. To accept misunderstanding, persecutions, before we break with what we believe in, before there is a break between life and convictions: that is coherence. Here we find perhaps the most intimate nucleus of fidelity.

But fidelity must stand the most difficult test: perseverance. That is the fourth dimension of fidelity: perseverance. It is easy to be coherent for a day or even for a few days. It is difficult, however important, to be coherent through an entire life of faith. It is easy to be coherent at the hour of elation, but difficult in the hour of tribulation. And we can call it fidelity when it lasts a lifetime.

The "fiat" of Mary at the Annunciation finds its fulfillment in the "fiat" at the foot of the cross. To be faithful is to remain faithful in private to what we proclaimed in public.

("A Call to Fidelity," Mexico City, Jan. 26, 1979)

PRAYER: DECEMBER 20

God of love and mercy,
help us to follow the example of Mary,
always ready to do your will.
At the message of an angel
she welcomed your eternal Son
and, filled with the light of your Spirit,
she became the temple of your Word,
who lives and reigns with you and the Holy Spirit,
one God, for ever and ever. Amen.

Article 10

United themselves to the redemptive obedience of Jesus, who placed his will into the Father's hands, let them faithfully fulfill the duties proper to their various circumstances of life. Let them also follow the poor and crucified Christ, witness to him even in difficulties and persecutions.

Theme: Discovering the Will of God in Life's Circumstance

Gospel: Mt 26:36–42

Then Jesus came with them to a small estate called Gethsemane, and he said to his disciples, "Stay here while I go over there to pray." He took Peter and the two sons of Zebedee with him. And sadness came over him, and great distress. The he said to them, "My soul is sorrowful to the point of death. Wait here and keep awake with me." And going on a little further he fell on his face and prayer. "My Father," he said, "if it is possible, let this pass me by. Nevertheless, let it be as you, not I, would have it." He came back to the disciples and found them sleeping, and he said to Peter, "So you have not the strength to keep awake with me one hour? You should be awake, and praying not to be put to the test. The spirit is willing, but the flesh is weak." Again, a second time, he went away and prayed: "My Father," he said, "if this cup cannot pass by without my drinking it, your will be done!"

New Testament: Phil 2:5–11

In your minds you must be the same as Christ Jesus:
His state was divine,
yet he did not cling
to his equality with God
but emptied himself
to assume the condition of a slave,
and became as men are,
and being as all men are,

he was humbler yet,
even to accepting death,
death on a cross.
But God raised him high
and gave him the name
which is above all other names
so that all beings
in the heavens, on earth and in the underworld
should bend the knee at the name of Jesus
and that every tongue should acclaim
Jesus Christ as Lord,
to the glory of God the Father.

OLD TESTAMENT: IS 52:13–53:12

See, my servant will prosper,
he shall be lifted up, exalted, rise to great heights.
As the crowds were appalled on seeing him
—so disfigured did he look
that he seemed no longer human—
so will the crowds be astonished at him,
and kings stand speechless before him;
for they shall see something never told
and witness something never heard before:
"Who could believe what we have heard,
and to whom has the power of Yahweh been revealed?"
Like a sapling he grew up in front of us,
like a root in arid ground.
Without beauty, without majesty (we saw him),
no looks to attract our eyes,
a thing despised and rejected by men,
a man of sorrows and familiar with suffering,
a man to make people screen their faces,
he was despised and we took no account of him.
And yet ours were the sufferings he bore,
ours the sorrows he carried.
But we, we thought of him as someone punished,
struck by God, and brought low.
Yet he was pierced through for our faults,
crushed for our sins.

On him lies a punishment that brings us peace,
and through his wounds we are healed.
We had all gone astray like sheep,
each taking his own way,
and Yahweh burdened him
with the sins of all of us.
Harshly dealt with, he bore it humbly,
he never opened his mouth,
like a lamb that is led to the slaughter-house,
like a sheep that is dumb before its shearers
never opening its mouth.
By force and by law he was taken,
would anyone plead his cause?
Yes, he was torn away from the land of the living,
for our faults struck down in death.
They gave him a grace with the wicked,
a tomb with the rich,
though he had done no wrong
and there had been no perjury in his mouth.
Yahweh has been pleased to crush him with suffering.
If he offers his life in atonement,
he shall see his heirs, he shall have a long life
and through him what Yahweh wishes will be done.
His soul's anguish over
he shall see the light and be content.
By his sufferings shall my servant justify many,
taking their faults on himself.
Hence I will grant whole hordes for his tribute,
he shall divide the spoil with the mighty,
for surrendering himself to death
and letting himself to be taken for a sinner,
while he was bearing the faults of many
and praying all the time for sinners.

also Is 42:1–9
    Is 49:1–6
    Is 50:4–11

PSALM 25

To you, O Lord, I lift up my soul.
I trust you, let me not be disappointed,
do not let my enemies triumph.
Those who hope in your shall not be disappointed,
but only those who wantonly break faith.

Lord, make me know your ways.
Lord, teach me your paths.
Make me walk in your truth, and teach me:
for you are God my savior.

In you I hope all day long
because of your goodness, O Lord.
Remember your mercy, Lord,
and the love you have shown from of old.
Do not remember the sins of my youth.
in your love remember me.

The Lord is good and upright.
He shows the path to those who stray,
he guides the humble in the right path,
he teaches his way to the poor.

His ways are faithfulness and love
for those who keep his covenant and law.
Lord, for the sake of your name
forgive my guilt, for it is great.
If anyone fears the Lord
he will show him the path he should choose.
His soul shall live in happiness
and his children shall possess the land.
The Lord's friendship is for those who revere him
to them he reveals his covenant.

My eyes are always on the Lord,
for he rescues my feet from the snare.
Turn to me and have mercy
for I am lonely and poor.

Relieve the anguish of my heart
and set me free from my distress.

See my affliction and my toil
and take all my sins away.

See how many are my foes,
how violent their hatred for me.
Preserve my life and rescue me.
Do not disappoint me, you are my refuge.
May innocence and uprightness protect me:
for my hope is in you, O Lord.

Redeem Israel, O God, from all its distress.

WRITING OF FRANCIS: 2LF 39–40

We must observe the commands and counsels of our Lord Jesus Christ. We must also deny ourselves and place our bodies under yoke of service and holy obedience, as each one has promised to the Lord.

alsoSalVirt 3, 13–11

WRITING OF CLARE: 5L 5–12

Our labor here is brief, but the reward is eternal. Do not be disturbed by the clamor of the world, which passes like a shadow. Do not let the false delights of a deceptive world deceive you. Close your ears to the whisperings of hell and bravely oppose its onslaughts. Gladly endure whatever goes against you and do not let others demand it. Offer faithfully what you have vowed to God, and He shall reward you.

O dearest one, look up to heaven, which calls us on, and take up the Cross and follow Christ Who has gone on before us: for through HIm we shall enter into His glory after many and diverse tribulations. Love God from the depths of your heart and Jesus, His Son, Who was crucified for us sinners. Never let the thoughts of Him leave your mind but meditate on the mysteries of the Cross and the anguish of His mother as she stood beneath the Cross.

also TCl 7

FRANCISCAN SOURCES: 3STIG

(On Mount Alverna) St. Francis, sometime before dawn, began to pray outside the entrance of his cell, turning his face toward the east. And he prayed in this way: "My Lord Jesus Christ, I pray You to grant me two graces before I die: the first is that during my life I may feel in my soul and in my body, as much as possible, the pain which You, dear Jesus, sustained in the hour of Your most bitter Passion. The second is that I may feel in my heart, as much as possible, that excessive love with which You, O Son of God, were inflamed in willingly enduring such suffering for us sinners."

And remaining for a long time in that prayer, he understood that God would grant it to him, and that it would soon be conceded to him to feel those things as much as is possible for a mere creature.

Having received this promise, St. Francis began to contemplate with intense devotion the Passion of Christ and His infinite charity. And the fervor of his devotion increased so much within him that he utterly transformed himself into Jesus through love and compassion. And while he was thus inflaming himself in this contemplation, on that same morning he saw coming down from heaven a Seraph with six resplendent and flaming wings. As the Seraph, flying swiftly, came closer to St. Francis, so that he could perceive Him clearly, he noticed that He had the likeness of a Crucified Man, and His wings were so disposed that two wings extended above His head, two were spread out to fly, and the other two covered His entire body.

On seeing this, St. Francis was very much afraid, and at the same time he was filled with joy and grief and amazement. He felt intense joy from the friendly look of Christ, who appeared to him in a very familiar way and gazed at him very kindly. But on the other hand, seeing Him nailed to the Cross, he felt boundless grief and compassion. Next, he was greatly amazed at such an astounding and extraordinary vision, for he knew well that the affliction of suffering is not in accord with the immortality of the angelic Seraph. And while he was marveling thus, He who was appearing to him revealed to him that this vision was shown to him by Divine Providence in this particular form in order that he should understand that he was to be utterly transformed into the direct likeness of Christ Crucified, not by physical martyrdom, but by enkindling of the mind....

Now when, after a long time and a secret conversation, this wonderful vision disappeared, it left a most intense ardor and flame of divine love in the heart of St. Francis, and it left a marvelous image and imprint of the Passion of Christ in his flesh.

VATICAN II DOCUMENT: LG 41F–G

In a special way also, those who are weighed down by poverty, infirmity, sickness and other hardships should realize that they are united to Christ, who suffers for the salvation of the world; let those feel the same who suffer persecution for the sake of justice, those whom the Lord declared blessed in the Gospel and whom "the God of all grace, who has called us to his eternal glory in Christ Jesus, will himself restore, establish, strengthen and settle" (1 Pet 5:10).

Accordingly all Christians, in the conditions, duties and circumstances of their life and through all these, will sanctify themselves more and more if they receive all things with faith from the hand of the heavenly Father and cooperate with the divine will, thus showing forth in that temporal service the love with which God has loved the world.

also LG 42d

PAPAL STATEMENT: SD 22B

The motif of suffering and glory has a strictly evangelical characteristic, which becomes clear by reference to the Cross and the Resurrection. The Resurrection became, first of all, the manifestation of glory, which corresponds to Christ's being lifted up through the Cross. If, in fact, the Cross was to human eyes Christ's emptying of himself, at the same time it was in the eyes of God his being lifted up. On the Cross, Christ attained and fully accomplished his mission: by fulfilling the will of the Father, he at the same time fully realized himself. In weakness he manifested his power, and in humiliation he manifested all his messianic greatness. Are not all the words he uttered during his agony on Golgotha a proof of this greatness, and especially his words concerning the perpetrators of his crucifixion: "Father, forgive them for they know not what they do"? To those who share in Christ's sufferings these words present themselves with the power of a supreme example. Suffering is also an invitation to manifest the moral greatness of man, his spiritual maturity. Proof of this has been given, down through the generations, by the martyrs and confessors of Christ, faithful to the words: "And do not fear those who kill the body, but cannot kill the soul."

also Eft 51
   ET 29–31

PRAYER: PASSION (PALM) SUNDAY

> Almighty, every-living God,
> you have given the human race Jesus Christ our Savior
> as a model of humility.
> He fulfilled your will
> by becoming man and giving his life on the cross.
> Help us to bear witness to you
> by following his example of suffering
> and make us worthy to share in his resurrection.
> We ask this through Christ our Lord. Amen.

Article 11

Trusting in the Father, Christ chose for himself and his mother a poor and humble life, even though he valued created things attentively and lovingly. Let the Secular Franciscans seek a proper spirit of detachment from temporal goods by simplifying their own material needs. Let them be mindful that according to the gospel they are stewards of the goods received for the benefit of God's children.

Thus, in the spirit of the "Beatitudes," and as pilgrims and strangers on their way to the home of the Father, they should strive to purify their hearts from every tendency and yearning for possession and power.

THEME: EMBRACING EVANGELICAL POVERTY AND DETACHMENT

GOSPEL: LK 12:22–34

Then he said to his disciples, "That is why I am telling you not to worry about your life and what you are to eat, not about body and how you are to clothe it. For life means more than food, and the body more than clothing. Think of the ravens. They do not sow or reap, they have no storehouses and no barns, yet God feeds them. And how much more are you worth than the birds! Can any of you, for all his worrying, add a single cubit to his span of life? If the smallest things, therefore, are outside your control, why worry about the rest? Think of the flowers, they never have to spin or weave, yet, I assure you, not even Solomon in all his regalia was robed like one of these. Now if that is how God clothes the grass in the field which is there today and thrown into the furnace tomorrow, how much more will he look after you, you men of little faith! But you, you must not set your hearts on things to eat and things to drink, nor must you worry. It is the pagans of this world who set their hearts on all these things. Your Father well knows you need them. No, set your hearts on his kingdom, and these other things will be given you as well.

"There is no need to be afraid, little flock, for it has pleased your Father to give you the kingdom.

"Sell your possessions and give alms. Get yourself purses that do not wear out, treasure that will not fail you, in heaven where no thief can reach it and no moth destroy it. For where your treasure is, there will your heart be also."

also Mt 5:3–12
  Mk 17–31
  Lk 12:22–34

NEW TESTAMENT: 2 COR 8:9

Remember how generous the Lord Jesus was: he was rich, but he became poor for your sake, to make you rich out of his poverty.

also Jas 2:5

OLD TESTAMENT: ZEPH 2:3; 3:12–13

> Seek Yahweh,
> all you humble of the earth,
> who obey his commands.
> Seek integrity,
> seek humility:
> you may perhaps find shelter
> on the day of the anger of Yahweh.
> When that day comes
> in your midst I will leave
> a humble and lowly people,
> and those who are left in Israel will see refuge
>   in the name of Yahweh.
> They will do no wrong,
> will tell no lies,
> and the perjured tongue will no longer
> be found in their mouths.
> But they will be able to graze and rest
> with no one to disturb them.

Psalm 34

I will bless the Lord at all times,
his praise always on my lips,
in the Lord my soul shall make its boast.
The humble shall hear and be glad.

Glorify the Lord with me.
Together let us praise his name.
I sought the Lord and he answered me,
from all my terrors he set me free.

Look toward him and be radiant,
let your faces not be abashed.
This poor man called, the Lord heard him
and rescued him from all his distress.

The angel of the Lord is encamped
around those who revere him, to rescue them.
Taste and see that the Lord is good.
He is happy who seeks refuge in him.

Revere the Lord, you his saints.
They lack nothing, those who revere him.
Strong lions suffer want and go hungry
but those who seek the Lord lack no blessing.

Come,. children, and hear me
that I may teach you the fear of the Lord.
Who is he who longs for life
and many days, to enjoy his prosperity?

Then keep your tongue from evil
and your lips from seeking deceit.
Turn aside from evil and do good,
seek and strive after peace.

The Lord turns his face against the wicked
to destroy their remembrance from the earth.
The Lord turns his eyes to the just
and his ears to their appeal.

They call and the Lord hears

and rescues them in all their distress.
The Lord is close to the broken-hearted,
those whose spirit is crushed he will save.

Many are the trials of the just man
but from them all the Lord will rescue him.
He will keep guard over all his bones,
not one of his bones shall be broken.

Evil brings death to the wicked,
those who hate the good are doomed.
He ransoms the souls of his servants.
Those who hide in him shall not be condemned.

WRITING OF FRANCIS: 2R 6:1–6

The brothers shall not acquire anything as their own, neither a
house nor a place not anything at all. Instead, as pilgrims and
strangers in this world who serve the Lord in poverty and humility,
let them go begging for alms with full trust. Nor should they feel
ashamed since the Lord made Himself poor for us in this world. This
is that summit of highest poverty which has established you, my
most beloved brothers, as heirs and kings of the kingdom of heaven,
it has made you poor in the things (of this world) but exalted you in
virtue. Let this be your portion, which leads into the land of the living. Dedicating yourself totally to this, my most beloved brothers,
do not wish to have anything else forever under heaven for the sake
of our Lord Jesus Christ.

WRITING OF CLARE: 1L 15–17,19–30

O blessed poverty, who bestows eternal riches
on those who love and embrace her!
O holy poverty, to whose who posses and desire you
God promises the kingdom of heaven
and offers, indeed, eternal glory and blessed life!
O God-centered poverty, whom the Lord Jesus Christ
Who ruled and now rules heaven and earth,
Who spoke and things were made,
condescended to embrace before all else!

If so great and good a Lord, then, on coming into the Virgin's womb, chose to appear despised, needy, and poor in this world, so that people who were in utter poverty and want and in absolute need of heavenly nourishment might become rich (cf. 2 Cor 8:9) in Him by possessing the kingdom of heaven, then rejoice and be glad (Hab 3:18)! Be filled with a remarkable happiness and a spiritual joy! Contempt of the world has pleased You more than [its] honors, poverty more than earthly riches, and You have sought to store up greater treaures in heaven rather than on earth, where rust does not consume nor moth destroy nor thieves break in and steal (Mt 6:20). Your reward, then, is very great in heaven (Mt 5:12)! And You truly have merited to be called a sister, a spouse, and mother (2 Cor 11:2; Mt 12:50) of the Son of the Father of the Most High and of the glorious Virgin.

You know, I am sure, that the kingdom of heaven is promised and given by the Lord only to the poor (Cf. Mt 5:3): for he who loves temporal things loses the fruit of love....

You also know that one who is clothed cannot fight with another who is naked, because he is more quickly thrown who gives his adversary a chance to get hold of him; and that one who lives in the glory of earth cannot rule with Christ in heaven.

Again, [you kow] that is it easier for a camel to pass through the eye of a needle than for a rich man to enter the kingdom of heaven (Mt 19:24). Therefore, you have cast aside Your garments, that is, earthly riches, so that You might not be overcome by the one fighting aganist You, [and] that You might enter the kingdom of heaven through the straight path and the narrow gate (Mt 7:13–14).

> What a laudable exchange!
>> to leave the things of time for those of eternity,
>> to choose the things of heaven for the goods of earth,
>> to receive the hundred-fold in place of one,
>> and to possess a blessed and eternal life (Mt 19:29).

Franciscan Sources: 2Cel 55

While he was in this valley of tears, that blessed father considered the common wealth of the sons of men as trifles, and, ambitious for higher things, he longed for poverty with all his heart.

Looking upon poverty as especially dear to the Son of God, though it was spurned throughout the whole world, he sought to espouse in it perpetual charity. Therefore, after he had become a lover of her beauty, he not only left his father and mother, but even put aside all things, that he might cling to her more closely as his spouse and that they might be two in one spirit. Therefore he gathered her to himself with chaste embraces and not even for an hour did he allow himself not to be her husband. This, he would tell his sons, is the way to perfection, this the pledge and earnest of eternal riches. There was no one so desirous of gold as he was desirous of poverty, and no one so solicitous in guarding his treasure as he was solicitous in guarding this pearl of the Gospel. In this, above all, would his sight be offended, if he saw anything contrary to poverty in his brothers either at home or away from home. Indeed, from the very beginning of his religious life unto his death he was rich in having only a tunic, a cord, and drawers, and he had nothing else. His poor habit showed where he was laying up his riches. With this he went his way happy, secure, and confident, he rejoiced to exchange a perishable treasure for the hundred fold.

VATICAN II DOCUMENT: LG 42D,E

The Church bears in mind too, the apostle's admonition when calling the faithful to charity and exhorting them to have the same mind which Christ Jesus showed, who "emptied himself, taking the form of a servant... and became obedient unto death" (Phil 2: 7–8) and for our sakes "became poor, though he was rich" (2 Cor 8:9). Since the disciples must always imitate this love and humility of Christ and bear witness to it, Mother Church rejoices that she has within herself many men and women who pursue more closely the Savior's self-emptying and show it forth more clearly, by undertaking poverty with the freedom of God's sons, and renouncing their own will...

Therefore all the faithful are invited and obliged to holiness and the perfection of their own state of life. Accordingly let all of them see that they direct their affections rightly, lest they be hindered in their pursuit of perfect love by the use of worldly things and by an adherence to riches which is contrary to the spirit of evangelical poverty, following the apostle's advice: Let those who use this world not fix their abode in it, for the form of this world is passing away (of. 1 Cor 7:31).

also GS 69

PAPAL STATEMENT: RD 12

How very expressive in the matter of poverty are the words of the Second Letter to the Corinthians which constitute a concise synthesis of all that we hear on this then in the Gospel! "For you know the grace of our Lord Jesus Christ, that though he was rich, yet for your sake he became poor, so that by his poverty you might become rich." According to these words poverty actually enters into the interior structure of the redemptive grace of Jesus Christ. Without poverty it is not possible to understand the mystery of the gift of divinity to man, a gift which is accomplished precisely in Jesus Christ. For this reason also it is found at the very center of the Gospel, at the beginning of the message of the eight Beatitudes: "Blessed are the poor in spirit."

Evangelical poverty reveals to the eyes of the human soul the perspective of the whole mystery, "hidden for ages in God." Only those who are "poor" in this way are also interiorly capable of understanding the poverty of the one who is infinitely rich. The poverty of Christ conceals in itself this infinite richness of God, it is indeed an infallible expression of it. A richness, in fact, such as the Divinity itself, could not have been adequately expressed in any created good. It can be expressed only in poverty. Therefore it can be properly understood only by the poor, the poor in spirit. Christ, the God-man, is the first of these: he who "though he was rich became poor" is not only the teacher but also the spokesman and guarantor of that salvific poverty which corresponds to the infinite richness of God and to the inexhaustible power of his grace.

And thus it is also true—as the Apostle writes—that "by his poverty we have become rich." It is the teacher and spokesman of poverty which makes us rich. For this very reason he says to the young man of the Synoptic Gospels: "Sell what you possess and give.... and you will have treasure in heaven." In these words there is a call to enrich others through one's own poverty, but in the depths of this call there is hidden the testimony of the infinite richness of God which, transferred to the human soul in the mystery of grace, creates in man himself, precisely through poverty, a source for enriching others not comparable with any other resource of material goods, a source for bestowing gifts on others in the manner of God himself. This giving is accomplished in the context of the mystery of Christ, who "has made us rich by his poverty." We see how this process of enrichment unfolds in the pages of the Gospel, finding its culmination in the paschal event: Christ, the poorest in his death on the Cross, is also the one who enriches us infinitely with the fullness of new life, through the Resurrection.

Dear Brothers and Sisters, poor in spirit through your evangelical profession, receive into the whole of your life this salvific profile of the poverty of Christ. Day by day seek its ever greater development! Seek above all "the Kingdom of God and his righteousness" and the other things "shall be yours as well." May there be accomplished in you and through you the evangelical blessedness reserved for the poor, the poor in spirit!

also ES 54–55

Prayer: Twenty-fourth Sunday in Ordinary Time

> Father in heaven, Creator of all,
> look down upon your people in their moments of need,
> for you alone are the source of our peace.
> Bring us to the dignity which distinguishes
>   the poor in spirit
> and show us how great is the call to serve,
> that we may share in the peace of Christ
> who offered his life in the service of all.
> We ask this through Christ our Lord. Amen.

Article 12

Witnessing to the good yet to come and obliged to acquire purity of heart because of the vocation they have embraced, they should set themselves free to love God and their brothers and sisters.

THEME: SEEKING PURITY OF HEART

GOSPEL: JN 15:9–17

As the Father has loved me,
so I have loved you.
Remain in my love.
If you keep my commandments
you will remain in my love,
just as I have kept my Father's commandments
and remain in his love.
I have told you this
so that my joy may be in you
and your joy may be complete.
This is my commandment:
love one another,
as I have loved you.
A man can have no greater love
than to lay down his life for his friends.
You are my friends,
if you do what I command you.
I shall not call you servants any more,
because a servant does not know
his master's business;
I call you friends,
because I have made known to you
everything I have learnt from my Father.
You did not choose me,
no, I chose you,
and I commissioned you
to go out and bear fruit,
fruit that will last,
and then the Father will give you

anything you ask him in my name.
What I command you
is to love one another.

NEW TESTAMENT: ROM 12:1–2

Think of God's mercy, my brothers, and worship him, I beg you, in a way that is worthy of thinking beings, by offering your living bodies as a holy sacrifice, truly pleasing to God. Do not model yourselves on the behavior of the world around you, but let your behavior change, modeled by your new mind. This is the only way to discover the will of God and know what is good, what it is that God wants, what is the perfect thing to do.

also :9–11
    2 Pet 1:3–9

OLD TESTAMENT: SONG 8:6–7

Set me like a seal on your heart,
like a seal on your arm.
For love is strong as Death,
jealousy relentless as Sheol.
The flash of it is a flash of fire,
a flame of Yahweh himself.
Love no flood can quench,
no torrents drown.

PSALM 119A

They are happy whose life is blameless,
who follow God's law!
They are happy who do his will,
seeking him with all their hearts,
who never do anything evil
but walk in his ways.
You have laid down your precepts
to be obeyed with care.
May my footsteps be firm

to obey your statutes.
Then I shall not be put to shame
as I heed your commands.
I will thank you with an upright heart
as I learn your decrees.
I will obey your statutes:
do not forsake me.

WRITING OF FRANCIS: ADM 16

"Blessed are the pure of heart for they shall see God." The truly pure of heart are those who despise the things of earth and seek the things of heaven, and who never cease to adore and behold the Lord God living and true with a pure heart and soul.

also 1R 22
    2LF 10:1–3

WRITING OF CLARE: 1L 8–14

"When You have loved [Him], You shall be chaste; when You have touched [Him], You shall become pure; when you have accepted [Him], You shall be a virgin."
    Whose power is stronger,
    Whose generosity is more abundant,
    Whose appearance more beautiful,
    Whose love more tender,
    Whose courtesy more gracious.
    In Whose embrace You are already caught up;
    Who has adorned Your breast with precious stones
        And has placed priceless pearls in Your ears
        and has surrounded You with sparkling gems
        as though blossoms of springtime
        and placed on Your head "a golden crown
        as a sign [to all] of Your holiness."

Therefore, most beloved sister, or should I say, Lady worthy of great respect: because You are the spouse and mother and the sister of my Lord Jesus Christ (2 Cor 1:2; Mt 12:50), and have been adorned respendently with the sign of invioable virginity and most holy poverty: Be strengthened in the holy service which You have undertaken out of an ardent desire for the Poor Crucified, Who for the sake of all of us took upon Himself the Passion of the Cross (Heb 12:2) and delivered us from the power of the Prince of Darkness (Col 1:13) to whom we were enslaved because of the disobedience of our first parent, and so reconciled us to God the Father (2 Cor 5:18).

FRANCISCAN SOURCES: 1CEL 83

O how beautiful, how splendid, how glorious did he appear in the innocence of his life, in the simplicity of his words, in the purity of his heart, in his love for God, in his fraternal charity, in his ardent obedience, in his peaceful submission, in his angelic countenance! He was charming in his manners, serene by nature, affable in his conversation, most opportune in his exhortations, most faithful in what was entrusted to him, cautious in counsel, effective in business, gracious in all things. He was serene of mind, sweet of disposition, sober in spirit, raised up in contemplation, zealous in prayer, and in all things fervent. He was constant in purpose, stable in virtue, persevering in grace, and unchanging in all things. He was quick to pardon, slow to become angry, ready of wit, tenacious of memory, subtle in discussion, circumspect in choosing, and in all things simple. He was unbending with himself, understanding toward others, and discreet in all things.

also LM 5:3
    SP 86

VATICAN II DOCUMENT: GS 38

The Word of God, through whom all things were made, became man and dwelt among men: a perfect man, he entered world history, taking that history into himself and recapitulating it. He reveals to us that "God is love" (1 Jn 4:8) and at the same time teaches that the fundamental law of human perfection, and consequently of the transformation of the world, is the new commandment of love. He assures those who trust in the charity of God that the way of love is open to all men and that the effort to establish a universal brotherhood will not be in vain. This love is not something reserved for important matters, but must be exercised above all in the ordinary circumstances of daily life.

also AA 8b
    GS 24

PAPAL STATEMENT: RD 3

"Jesus looking upon him loved him" and said to him, "If you would be perfect, go, sell what you have, and give to the poor, and you will have treasure in heaven, and come, follow me." Even though we know that those words, addressed to the rich young man, were not accepted by the one being called, their content deserves to be carefully reflected upon, for they present the interior structure of a vocation.

"And Jesus looking upon him loved him." This is the love of the Redeemer: a love that flows from all the human and divine depths of the Redemption. This love reflects the eternal love of the Father, who "so loved the world that he gave his only Son, that whoever believes in him should not perish but have eternal life." The Son, invested with that love, accepted the mission from the Father in the Holy Spirit, and became the Redeemer of the world. The Father's love was revealed in the Son as redeeming love. It is precisely this love that constitutes the true price of the Redemption of man and the world. Christ's Apostles speak of the price of the Redemption with profound emotion: "You were ransomed... not with perishable things such as silver or gold, but with the precious blood of Christ, like that of a lamb without blemish or spot," writes Saint Peter. And Saint Paul states: "You were bought with a price."

The call to the way of the evangelical counsels springs from the interior encounter with the love of Christ, which is a redeeming love. Christ calls precisely through this love of his. In the structure of a vocation, the encounter with this love becomes something specifically personal. When Christ "looked upon you and loved you," calling each one of you... that redeeming love of his was directed towards a particular person, and at the same time it took on a spousal character: it became a love of choice. This love embraces the whole person, soul and body, whether man or woman, in that person's unique and unrepeatable personal "I." The One who, given eternally to the Father, "gives" himself in the mystery of the Redemption, has now called man in order that he in his turn should give himself entirely to the world of the Redemption.... Surely it is to precisely this call that Saint Paul's words can be applied: "Do you not know that your body is a temple of the Holy Spirit...? You are not your own, you were bought with a price."

Yes, Christ's love has reached each one of you with that same price of Redemption. As a consequence of this, you have realized that you are not your own, but belong to Christ. This new awareness was the fruit of Christ's "loving look" in the secret of your heart. You replied to that look by choosing him who first chose each one of you, calling you with the measurelessness of his redeeming love. Since he calls "by name," his call always appeals to human freedom. Christ says: "If you wish..." And the response to this call is, therefore, a free choice. You have chosen Jesus of Nazareth, the Redeemer of the world, by choosing the way that he has shown you.

PRAYER: TENTH SUNDAY IN ORDINARY TIME

> Father in heaven,
> words cannot measure the boundaries of love
> for those born to new life in Christ Jesus.
> Raise us beyond the limits this world imposes,
> so that we may be free to love as Christ teaches
> and find our joy in your glory.
> We ask this through Christ our Lord. Amen.

Article 13

As the Father sees in every person the features of his Son, the firstborn of many brothers and sisters, so the Secular Franciscans with a gentle and courteous spirit accept all people as a gift of the Lord and an image of Christ.

A sense of community will make them joyful and ready to place themselves on an equal basis with all people, especially with the lowly for whom they shall strive to create conditions of life worthy of people redeemed by Christ.

THEME: BUILDING A UNIVERSAL COMMUNITY OF DIGNITY AND EQUALITY

GOSPEL: MT 25:31–40

When the Son of Man comes in his glory with all his angels, then he will take his seat on his throne of glory. All the nations will be assembled before him and he will separate men from one another as the shepherd separates sheep from goats. He will place the sheep on his right hand and the goats on his left. Then the King will say to those on his right hand, "Come, you whom my Father has blessed, take for your heritage the kingdom prepared for you since the foundation of the world. For I was hungry and you gave me food, I was thirsty and you gave me drink, I was a stranger and you made me welcome, naked and you clothed me, sick and you visited me, in prison and you came to see me." Then the virtuous will say to him in reply, "Lord, when did we see you hungry and feed you, or thirsty and give you drink? When did we see you a stranger and make you welcome, naked and clothe you, sick or in prison and go to see you?" And the King will answer, "I tell you solemnly, in so far as you did this to one of the least of these brothers of mine, you did it to me." Next he will say to those on his left hand, "Go away from Me, with your curse upon you, to the eternal fire prepared for the devil and his angels. For I was hungry and you never gave me food, I was thirsty and you never gave me anything to drink, I was a stranger and you never made me welcome, naked and you never clothed me, sick and in prison and you never visited me." Then it will be their turn to ask, "Lord, when did we see you hungry or thirsty, a stranger or naked, sick or in prison, and did not come to your help?" Then he will answer, "I tell you solemnly, in so far as you neglected to do this to one of the least of these, you neglected to do it to me." And they will go away to eternal punishment, and the virtuous to eternal life.

NEW TESTAMENT: ROM 12:9–18

Do not let your love be a pretense, but sincerely prefer good to evil. Love each other as much as brothers should, and have a profound respect for each other. Work for the Lord with untiring effort and with great earnestness of spirit. if you have hope, this will make you cheerful. Do not give up if trials come, and keep on praying. If any of the saints are in need you must share with them, and you should make hospitality your special care. Bless those who persecute you: never curse them, bless them. Rejoice with those who rejoice and be sad with those in sorrow. Treat everyone with equal kindness, never be condescending but real friends with the poor. Do not allow yourself to become self-satisfied. Never repay evil with evil but let everyone see that you are interested only in the highest ideals. Do all you can to live at peace with everyone.

also Col 3:12–17

OLD TESTAMENT: ZEPH 3:16–20

When that day comes, word will come to Jerusalem:
Zion, have no fear,
do not let your hands fall limp.
Yahweh your God is in your midst,
a victorious warrior.
He will exult with joy over you,
he will renew you by his love,
he will dance with shouts of joy for you
as on a day of festival.
I have taken away your misfortune,
no longer need you bear the disgrace of it.
I am taking action here and now
against your oppressors.

When that time comes I will rescue the lame,
and gather the strays,
and I will win them praise and renown
when I restore their fortunes.
When that time comes, I will be your guide,
when that time comes, I will gather you in,
I will give you praise and renown
among all the peoples of the earth
when I restore your fortunes under your own eyes:
says Yahweh.

PSALM 8

How great is your name, O Lord our God
through all the earth!
Your majesty is praised above the heavens,
on the lips of children and of babes
you have found praise to foil your enemy,
to silence the foe and the rebel.
When I see the heavens, the work of your hands,
the moon and the stars which you arranged,
what is man that you should keep him in mind,
mortal man that you care for him?
Yet you have made him little less than a god,
with glory and honor you crowned him,
gave him power over the works of your hand,
put all things under his feet.
All of them, sheep and cattle,
yes, even the savage beasts,
birds of the air, and fish
that make their way through the waters.
How great is your name, O Lord our God,
through all the earth!

WRITING OF FRANCIS: 1R 11:5–13

And they should love one another, as the Lord says: "This is my commandment: that you love one another as I have loved you." And let them express the love which they have for one another by their deeds, as the Apostle says: "Let us not love in word or speech, but in deed and in truth." And they should slander no one. Let them not murmur nor detract from others, for it is written: Gossip and detractors are detestable to God. And let them be modest, by showing meekness toward everyone. Let them not judge or condemn. And as the Lord says, they should not take notice of the little defects of others. Rather, they should reflect much more on their own (sins) in the bitterness of their soul. And let them strive to enter through the narrow gate, for the Lord says: "Narrow is the gate and hard the road that leads to life, and there are few who find it."

also 2R 3:10–11

WRITING OF CLARE: TCL 18

Loving one another with the charity of Christ, let the love you have in your hearts be shown outwardly in your deeds so that, compelled by such an example, the sisters may always grow in love of God and in charity for one another.

FRANCISCAN SOURCES: 2CEL 172

Since the strength of Francis' love made him a brother to all other creatures, it is not surprising that the charity of Christ made him more than a brother to those who are stamped with the image of their Creator. For he used to say that nothing is more important than the salvation of souls, and he often offered as proof the fact that the Only-begotten of God deigned to hang on the cross for souls. This accounts for his struggles at prayer, his tirelessness at preaching, his excess in giving examples. He did not consider himself a friend of Christ unless he loved the souls that Christ loved. And this was the main reason why he reverenced doctors so much, namely, because, as Christ's helpers, they exercised one office with him. He loved his brothers beyond measure with an affection that rose from his innermost being, because they were of the same household of faith and united by participation in an eternal inheritance according to the promise.

also 3Soc 57

VATICAN II DOCUMENT: GS 29

All men are endowed with a rational soul and are created in God's image, they have the same nature and origin and, being redeemed by Christ, they enjoy the same divine calling and destiny, there is here a basic equality between all men and it must be given ever greater recognition.

Undoubtedly not all men are alike as regards physical capacity and intellectual and moral powers. But forms of social or cultural discrimination in basic personal rights on the grounds of sex, race, color, social conditions, language or religion, must be curbed and eradicated as incompatible with God's design. It is regrettable that these basic personal rights are not yet being respected everywhere, as in the case with women who are denied the chance freely to choose a husband, or a state of life, or to have access to the same educational and cultural benefits as are available to men.

Furthermore, while there are rightful differences between people, their equal dignity as persons demands that we strive for fairer and more human conditions. Excessive economic and social disparity between individuals and peoples of the one human race is source of scandal and militates against social justice, equality, human dignity, as well as social and international peace.

It is up to public and private organizations to be at the service of the dignity and destiny of man, let them spare no effort to banish every vestige of social and political slavery and to safeguard basic human rights under every political system. And even if it takes a considerable time to arrive at the desired goal, these organizations should gradually be brought into harmony with spiritual realities, which are the most sublime of all.

also AA 8
  GS 24,27,32

PAPAL STATEMENT: PT 9–10,45

Any human society, if it is to be well-ordered and productive, must lay down as a foundation this principle, namely, that every being is a person, that is, his nature is endowed with intelligence and free will. Indeed, precisely because he is a person he has rights and obligations flowing directly and simultaneously from his very nature. And as these rights and obligations are universal and inviolable so they cannot in any way be surrendered.

If we look upon the dignity of the human person in the light of divinely revealed truth, we cannot help but esteem it far more highly, for men are redeemed by the blood of Christ, they are by grace the children and friends of God and heirs of eternal glory.

When the relations of human society are expressed in terms of rights and duties, men become conscious of spiritual values, understand the meaning and significance of truth, justice, charity and freedom, and become deeply aware that they belong to this world of values. Moreover, when moved by such concerns, they are brought to a better knowledge of the true God Who is personal and transcendent, and thus they make the ties that bind them to God the solid foundation and supreme criterion of their lives, both of that life which they live interiorly in the depths of their own souls and of that in which they are united to other men in society.

also RH 11
    LE 4
    DM 3
    PP 43, 47, 74

PRAYER: FOR THE PROGRESS OF PEOPLES

Father,
you have given all peoples one common origin,
and your will is to gather them as one family in yourself.
Fill the hearts of all people with the fire of your love
and the desire to ensure justice for all their brother
        and sisters.
By sharing the good things you give us
may we secure justice and equality for every living
        human being,
an end to all division,
and a human society built on love and peace.
We ask this through Christ our Lord. Amen.

Article 14

Secular Franciscans, together with all people of good will, are called to build a more fraternal and evangelical world so that the kingdom of God may be brought about more effectively. Mindful that anyone "who follows Christ, the perfect man, becomes more of a man himself," let them exercise their responsibilities competently in the Christian spirit of service.

THEME: ACTIVELY PROCLAIMING THE KINGDOM OF GOD (EVANGELIZATION)

GOSPEL: MT 7:21–25

It is not those who say to me, "Lord, Lord," who will enter the kingdom of heaven, but the person who does the will of my Father in heaven. When the day comes many will say to me, "Lord, Lord, did we not prophesy in your name, cast out demons in your name, work many miracles in your name?" Then I shall tell them to their faces: I have never known you, away from me, you evil men!

Therefore, everyone who listens to these words of mine and acts on them will be like a sensible man who built his house on rock. Rain came down, floods rose, gales blew and hurled themselves against that house, and it did not fall: it was founded on rock.

also Mt 10:7–20

NEW TESTAMENT: JAS 2:14–23

Take the case, my brothers, of someone who has never done a single good act but claims that he has faith. Will that faith save him? If one of the brothers or one of the sisters is in need of clothes and has not enough food to live on, and one of you says to them, "I wish you well, keep yourself warm and eat plenty," without giving them these bare necessities of life, then what good is that? Faith is like that: if good works do not go with it, it is quite dead.

This is the way to talk to people of that kind: "You say you have faith and I have good deeds, I will prove to you that I have faith by showing you my good deeds—now you prove to me that you have faith without any good deed to show. You believe in the one God— that is creditable enough, but the demons have the same belief, and they tremble with fear. Do realize, you senseless man, that faith without good deeds is useless. You surely know that Abraham our father was justified by his deed, because he offered his son Isaac on the altar? There you see it: faith and deeds were working together, his faith became perfect by what he did. This is what scripture really means when it says: Abraham put his faith in God, and this was counted as making him justified, and that is why he was called 'the friend of God.'"

also 2 Tim 4:1–5

OLD TESTAMENT: IS 52:7–10

How beautiful on the mountains,
are the feet of one who brings good news,
who heralds peace, brings happiness,
proclaims salvation,
and tells Zion,
"Your God is king!"
Listen! Your watchmen raise their voices,
they shout for joy together,
for they see Yahweh face to face,
as he returns to Zion.
Break into shouts of joy together,
you ruins of Jerusalem,
for Yahweh is consoling his people,
redeeming Israel.
Yahweh bears his holy arm
in the sight of the nations,
and all the ends of the earth shall see
the salvation of our God.

also Is 40:9–11

PSALM 96

O sing a new song to the Lord,
sing to the Lord, all the earth.
O sing to the Lord, bless his name.

Proclaim his help day by day,
tell among the nations his glory
and his wonders among all the peoples.

The Lord is great and worthy of praise,
to be feared above all gods,
the gods of the heathens are naught.

It was the Lord who made the heavens
his are majesty and state and power
and splendor in his holy place.

Give the Lord, you families of peoples,
give the Lord glory and power,
give the Lord the glory of his name.

Bring an offering and enter his courts
worship the Lord in his temple.
O earth, tremble before him.

Proclaim to the nations: "God is king."
The world he made firm in its place,
he will judge the peoples in fairness.

Let the heavens rejoice and earth be glad,
let the sea and all within it thunder praise,
let the land and all it bears rejoice,
all the trees of the wood shout for joy

at the presence of the Lord for he comes:
he comes to rule the earth.
With justice he will rule the world,
he will judge the people with his truth.

WRITING OF FRANCIS: 1R 16:5–11

As for the brothers who go, they can live spiritually among (the

Saracens and nonbelievers) in two ways. One way is not to engage in arguments or disputes, but to be subject to every human creature for God's sake and to acknowledge that they are Christians. Another way is to proclaim the word of God when they see it pleases the Lord, so that they believe in the all-powerful God—Father, Son, and Holy Spirit—the Creator of all, in the Son Who is the Redeemer and Savior, and that they be baptized and become Christians, because whoever has not been born again of water and the Holy Spirit cannot enter into the kingdom of God.

They can say to (the Saracens) and to others these and other things which will have pleased the Lord, for the Lord says in the Gospel: "Everyone who acknowledges me before men I will also acknowledge before my Father Who is in heaven." And: "Whoever is ashamed of me and my words, the Son of Man will also be ashamed of him when He comes in His majesty and that of the Father and the angels."

And all the brothers, wherever they may be, should remember that they gave themselves and abandoned their bodies to the Lord Jesus Christ. And for love of Him, they must make themselves vulnerable to their enemies, both visible and invisible, because the Lord says: "Whoever loses his life for my sake will save it in eternal life."

WRITING OF CLARE: TCL 6

The Lord Himself not only has set us as an example and mirror for others, but also for our own sisters whom the Lord has called to our way of life, so that they in turn will be mirror and example to those living in the world. Since, therefore, the Lord has called us to such great things, that those who are to be models and mirrors for others may behold themselves in us, we are truly bound to bless and praise the Lord and to be strengthened constantly in Him to do good. Therefore, if we have lived according to the form of life given us, we shall, by very little effort, leave others a noble example and gain the prize of eternal happiness.

FRANCISCAN SOURCES: 1CEL 29

At this same time also, when another good man had entered their religion, their number rose to eight. Then the blessed Francis

called them all together, and telling them many things concerning
the kingdom of God, the contempt of the world, the renunciation of
their own will, and the subduing of their own body, he separated
them into four groups of two each and said to them: "Go, my dearest
brothers, two by two into the various parts of the world, announcing to men peace and repentance unto the forgiveness of sins, and
be patient in tribulation, confident that the Lord will fulfill his purpose and his promise. To those who put questions to you, reply
humbly, bless those who persecute you, give thanks to those who
injure you and calumniate you, because for these things there is
prepared for you an eternal kingdom."

VATICAN II DOCUMENT: AA 2

The Church was founded to spread the kingdom of Christ over
all the earth for the glory of God the Father, to make all men partakers in redemption and salvation, and through them to establish
the right relationship of the entire world to Christ. Every activity of
the Mystical Body with this in view goes by the name of "apostolate"; the Church exercises it through all its members, though in
various ways. In fact, the Christian vocation is, of its nature, a vocation to the apostolate as well. In the organism of a living body no
member plays a purely passive party, sharing in the life of the body
it shares at the same time in its activity. The same is true for the
body of Christ, the Church: "the whole Body achieves full growth in
dependence on the full functioning of each part" (Eph 4:16).
Between the members of this body there exists, further, such a
unity and solidarity (cf. Eph 4:16) that a member who does not
work at the growth of the body to the extent of his possibilities
must be considered useless both to the Church and to himself.

In the Church there is a diversity of ministry but unity of mission. To the apostles and their successors Christ has entrusted the
office of teaching, sanctifying and governing in his name and by his
power. But the laity are made to share in the priestly prophetical
and kingly office of Christ: they have therefore, in the Church and
in the world, their own assignment in the mission of the whole
People of God. In the concrete, their apostolate is exercised when
they work at the evangelization and sanctification of men, it is exercised too when they endeavor to have the Gospel spirit permeate
and improve the temporal order, going about it in a way that bears

clear witness to Christ and helps forward the salvation of men. The characteristic of the lay state being a life led in the midst of the world and of secular affairs, laymen are called by God to make of their apostolate, through the vigor of their Christian spirit, a leaven in the world.

also LG 36
  AG 11
  GS 41, 43a–b, 72, 93

PAPAL STATEMENT: EN 21

Above all the Gospel must be proclaimed by witness. Take a Christian or a handful of Christians who, in the midst of their own community, show their capacity for understanding and acceptance, their sharing of life and destiny with other people, their solidarity with the efforts of all for whatever is noble and good. Let us suppose that, in addition, they radiate in an altogether simple and unaffected way their faith in values that go beyond current values, and their hope in something that is not seen and that one would not dare to imagine. Through this warless witness these Christians stir up irresistible questions in the hearts of those who see how they live: Why are they like this? Why do they live this way? What or who is it that inspires them? Why are they in our midst? Such a witness is already a silent proclamation of the Good News and a very powerful and effective one. Here we have an initial act of evangelization. The above questions when asked, will discover whether they are people to whom Christ has never been proclaimed, or baptized people who do not practice, or people who live as nominal Christians but according to principles that are in no way Christian, or people who are seeking, and not without suffering, something or someone whom they sense but cannot name. Other questions will arise, deeper and more demanding ones, questions which involve presence, sharing, solidarity, and which is an essential element, and generally the first one, in evangelization.

All Christians are called to this witness, and in this way they can be real evangelizers.

also EN 26, 41
  PP 75, 81

PRAYER: FOR THE SPREAD OF THE GOSPEL, B

Father,
you will your Church to be the sacrament of salvation
         for all peoples.
Make us feel more urgently
the call to work for the salvation of all,
until you have made us all one people.
Inspire the hearts of all your people
to continue the saving work of Christ everywhere
until the end of the world.
Grant this through Christ our Lord. Amen.

Article 15

Let them individually and collectively be in the forefront in promoting justice by the testimony of their human lives and their courageous initiatives. Especially in the field of public life, they should make definite choices in harmony with their faith.

THEME: PROMOTING JUSTICE
GOSPEL: MT 5:38–48

You have learnt how it was said: Eye for eye and tooth for tooth. But I say this to you: offer the wicked man no resistance. On the contrary, if anyone hits you on the right cheek, offer him the other as well, if a man takes you to law and would have your tunic, let him have your cloak as well. And if anyone orders you to go one mile, go two miles with him. Give to anyone who asks, and if anyone wants to borrow, do not turn him away.

You have learnt how it was said: You must love your neighbor and hate your enemy. But I say this to you: love your enemies and pray for those who persecute you, in this way you will be sons of your Father in heaven, for he causes his sun to rise on bad men as well as good, and his rain to fall on honest and dishonest men alike. For if you love those who love you, what right have you to claim any credit? Even the tax collectors do as much, do they not? And if you save your greetings for your brothers, are you doing anything exceptional? Even the pagans do as much, do they not? You must therefore be perfect just as your heavenly Father is perfect.

NEW TESTAMENT: COL 3:9–17

You have stripped off your old behavior with your old self, and you have put on a new self which will progress toward true knowledge the more it is renewed in the image of its creator, and in that image there is no room for distinction between Greek and Jew, between the circumcised or the uncircumcised, or between barbarian and Scythian, slave and free man. There is only Christ: he is everything and he is in everything.

You are God's chosen race, his saints, he loves you, and you should be clothed in sincere compassion, in kindness and humility, gentleness and patience. Bear with one another, forgive each other as soon as a quarrel begins. The Lord has forgiven you, now you must do the same. Over all these clothes, to keep them together and complete them, put on love. And may the peace of Christ reign in your hearts, because it is for this that you were called together as parts of one body. Always be thankful. Let the message of Christ, in all its richness, find a home with you. Teach each other, and advise each other, in all wisdom. With gratitude in your hearts sing psalms and hymns and inspired songs to God, and never say or do anything except in the name of the Lord Jesus, giving thanks to God the Father through him.

OLD TESTAMENT: IS 58:6–14

Is not this the sort of fasting that pleases me
—it is the Lord Yahweh who speaks—
to break unjust fetters
and undo the thongs of the yoke,
to let the oppressed go free,
and break every yoke,
to share your bread with the hungry,
and shelter the homeless poor,
to clothe the man you see to be naked
and not turn from your own kin?
Then will your light shine like the dawn
and your wound be quickly healed over.
Your integrity will go before you
and the glory of Yahweh behind you.
Cry, and Yahweh will answer,
call, and he will say, "I am here."
If you do away with the yoke,
the clenched fist, the wicked word,
if you give your bread to the hungry,
and relief to the oppressed,
your light will rise in the darkness,
and your shadows become like noon.
Yahweh will always guide you,
giving you relief in desert places.
He will give strength to your bones

and you shall be like a watered garden,
like a spring of water
whose waters never run dry.
You will rebuild the ancient ruins?
build up on the old foundations.
You will be called breach-mender,
Restorer of ruined houses.
If you refrain from trampling the sabbath,
and doing business on the holy day,
if you call the sabbath "Delightful,"
and the day sacred to Yahweh "Honorable,"
if you honor it by abstaining from travel,
from doing business and from gossip,
then you shall find your happiness in Yahweh
and I will lead you triumphant over the heights of the land
I will feed you on the heritage of Jacob your father.
For the mouth of Yahweh has spoken.

also Lv 19:11–18
      Job 29:11–17
      Mi 6:8

PSALM 15

Lord, who shall be admitted to your tent
and dwell in your holy mountain?
He who walks without fault,
he who acts with justice
and speaks the truth from his heart,
he who does not slander with his tongue,
he who does not wrong to his brothers,
who casts not slur on his neighbor,
who holds the godless in disdain,
but honors those who fear the Lord,
he who keeps his pledge, come what may,
who takes no interest on a loan
and accepts no bribes against the innocent.
Such a man will stand firm forever.

WRITING OF FRANCIS: 2LF 26–31

And let us love our neighbor as ourselves. And if there is anyone who does not wish to love them as himself, at least let him do no harm to them, but rather do good.

But those who have received the power to judge others should exercise judgment with mercy as they themselves desire to receive mercy from the Lord. For judgment will be without mercy for those who have not shown mercy.

Let us then have charity and humility, let us give alms since this washes our souls from the stains of (our) sins. For people lose everything they leave behind in this world, but they carry with them the rewards of charity and the alms which they gave, for which they will have a reward and a suitable remuneration from the Lord.

also Adm 8, 18, 24, 25

WRITING OF CLARE: 3L 4,7–10

I sigh with such happiness in the Lord because I know you see that you make up most wonderfully what is lacking both in me and in the other sisters in following the footprints of the poor and humble Jesus Christ.... I see, too, that by humility, the virtue of faith, and the strong arm of poverty, you have taken hold of that incomparable treasure hidden in the field of the world and in the hearts of men (cf. Mt 13:44), with which you have purchased that field of Him by Whom all things have been made from nothing. And, to use the words of the Apostle himself in their proper sense, I consider you a co-worker of God Himself (cf. 1 Cor 3:9; Rom 16:3) and a support of the weak members of his ineffable Body. Who is there, then, who would not encourage me to rejoice over such marvelous joys?

Therefore, dearly beloved, may you too always rejoice in the Lord (Phil 4:4). And may neither bitterness nor a cloud [of sadness] overwhelm you, O dearly beloved Lady in Christ, joy of the angels and crown of your sisters!

FRANCISCAN SOURCES: 1CEL 76

The father of the poor, the poor Francis, conforming himself to the poor in all things, was grieved when he saw some one poorer than himself, not because he longed for vainglory, but only from a feeling of compassion. And, though he was content with a tunic that was quite poor and rough, he very frequently longed to divide it with some poor person. But that this very rich poor man, drawn on by a great feeling of affection, might be able to help the poor in some way, he would ask the rich of this world, when the weather was cold, to give him a mantle or some furs. And when, out of devotion, they willingly did the most blessed father asked of them, he would say to them: "I will accept this from you with this understanding that you do not expect ever to have to back again." And when he met the first poor man, he would clothe him with what he had received with joy and gladness. He bore it very ill if he saw a poor person reproached or if he heard a curse hurled upon any creature by anyone.

also 2Cel 83–85
  3Soc 57–58

VATICAN II DOCUMENT: AA 7

That men, working in harmony, should renew the temporal order and make it increasingly more perfect: such is God's design for the world.

All that goes to make up the temporal order: personal and family values, culture, economic interests, the trades and professions, institutions of the political community, international relations, and so on, as well as their gradual development—all these are not merely helps to man's last end, they possess a value of their own, placed in them by God, whether considered individually or as parts of the integral temporal structure: "And God saw all that he had made and found it very good" (Gn 1:31). This natural goodness of theirs receives an added dignity from their relation with the human person, for whose use they have been created. And then, too, God has willed to gather together all that was natural, all that was supernatural, into a single whole in Christ, "so that in everything he would have the primacy" (Col 1:18). Far from depriving the temporal order of its autonomy, of its importance for human well-being, this design, on the contrary, increases its energy and excellence, raising it at the same time to the level of man's integral vocation here below.

In the course of history the use of temporal things has been tarnished by serious defects. Under the influence of original sin men have often fallen into very many errors about the true God, human nature and the principles of morality. As a consequence human conduct and institutions became corrupted, the human person itself held in contempt. Again in our own day not a few, putting an immoderate trust in the conquests of science and technology, turn off into a kind of idolatry of the temporal, they become the slaves of it rather than the masters.

It is the work of the entire Church to fashion men able to establish the proper scale of values on the temporal order and direct it toward God through Christ. Pastors have the duty to set forth clearly the principles concerning the purpose of creation and the use to be made of the world, and to provide moral and spiritual helps for the renewal of the temporal order in Christ.

Laymen ought to take on themselves as their distinctive task this renewal of the temporal order. Guided by the light of the Gospel and the mind of the Church, prompted by Christian love, they should act in this domain in a direct way and in their own specific manner. As citizens among citizens they must bring to their cooperation with others their own special competence, and act on their own responsibility, everywhere and always they have to see the justice of the kingdom of God. The temporal order is to be renewed in such a way that, while its own principles are fully respected, it is harmonized with the principles of the Christian life and adapted to the various conditions of times, places and peoples. Among the tasks of this apostolate Christian social action is preeminent. The Council desires to see it extended today to every sector of life, not forgetting the cultural sphere.

also AG 21
   GS 29, 30, 75

PAPAL STATEMENT: PT 146

Once again we exhort our children to take an active part in

public life, and to contribute towards the attainment of the common good of the entire human family as well as to that of their own country. They should endeavor, therefore, in the light of the Faith and with the strength of love, to ensure that the various institutions—whether economic, social, cultural or political in purpose—should be such as not to create obstacles, but rather to facilitate or render less arduous man's perfecting of himself both in the natural order as well as in the supernatural.

also LE 2, 8, 25
     PP 32, 47, 54, 74, 76, 81
     PT 146

Prayer: For Peace and Justice

> God our Father,
> you reveal that those who work for peace
> will be called your sons and daughters.
> Help us to work without ceasing
> for that justice
> which brings true and lasting peace.
> We ask this through Christ our Lord. Amen.

Article 16

Let them esteem work both as a gift and as a sharing in the creation, redemption, and service of the human community.

THEME: DEVELOPING PROPER ATTITUDES TOWARD WORK

GOSPEL: MT 25:14–30

The kingdom of heaven is like a man on his way abroad who summoned his servants and entrusted his property to them. To one he have five talents, to another two, to a third one, each in proportion to his ability. Then he set out. The man who had received the five talents promptly went and traded with them and made five more. The man who had received two made two more in the same way. But the man who had received one went off and dug a hole in the ground and hid his master's money. Now a long time after, the master of those servants came back and went through his accounts with them. The man who had received the five talents came forward bringing five more. "Sir," he said, "you entrusted me with five talents, here are five more that I have made." His master said to him, "Well done, good and faithful servant, you have shown you can be faithful in small things, I will trust you with greater, come and join in your master's happiness." Next the man with the two talents came forward. "Sir," he said, "you entrusted me with two talents, here are two more that I have made." His master said to him, "Well done, good and faithful servant, you have shown you can be faithful in small things, I will entrust you with greater, come and join in your master's happiness." Last came forward the man who had the one talent. "Sir," said he "I had heard you were a hard man, reaping where you have not sown and gathering where you have not scattered, so I was afraid, and I went off and hid your talent in the ground. Here it is, it was yours, you have it back." But his master answered him, "You wicked and lazy servant! So you knew that I reap where I have not sown and gather where I have not scattered? Well then, you should have deposited my money with the bankers, and on my return I would have recovered my capital with interest.

So now, take the talent from him and give it to the man who has the ten talents. For to everyone who has will be given more, and he will have more than enough, but from the man who has not, even what he has will be taken away. As for this good-for-nothing servant, throw him out into the dark, where there will be weeping and grinding of teeth."

NEW TESTAMENT: COL 3:17,23–25

Never say or do anything except in the name of the Lord Jesus, giving thanks to God the Father through him.... Whatever your work is, put your heart into it as if it were for the Lord and not for men, knowing that the Lord will repay you by making you his heirs. It is Christ the Lord that you are serving, anyone who does wrong will be repaid in kind and he does not favor one person more than another.

also Eph 6:7–8

OLD TESTAMENT: GN 1:26–2:3

God said, "Let us make man in our own image, in the likeness of ourselves, and let them be masters of the fish of the sea, the birds of heaven, the cattle, all the wide beasts and all the reptiles that crawl upon the earth."

> God created man in the image of himself,
> in the image of God he created him,
> male and female he created them.

God blessed them, saying to them, "Be fruitful, multiply, fill the earth and conquer it. Be masters of the fish of the sea, the birds of the heaven and all living animals on the earth." God said, "See, I give you all the seed-bearing plants that are upon the whole earth, and all the trees with seed-bearing fruit, this shall be your food. To all wild beasts, all birds of heaven and all living reptiles on the earth I give all the foliage of plants as food." And so it was. God saw all he had made, and indeed it was very good. Evening came and morning came: the sixth day.

Thus heaven and earth were completed with all their array. On the seventh day God completed the work he had been doing. He rested on the seventh day after all the work he had been doing. God blessed the seventh day and made it holy, because on that day he had rested after all his work of creating.

also Is 65:17–25

PSALM 127

If the Lord does not build the house,
in vain do its builders labor,
if the Lord does not watch over the city,
in vain does the watchman keep vigil.

In vain is your earlier rising,
your going later to rest,
you who toil for the bread you eat:
when he pours gifts on his beloved while they slumber.

Truly sons are a gift from the Lord,
a blessing, the fruit of the womb.
Indeed the sons of youth
are like arrows in the hand of a warrior.

O the happiness of the man
who has filled his quiver with these arrows!
He will have no cause for shame
when he disputes with his foes in the gateways.

WRITING OF FRANCIS: 2R 5:1–2

Those brothers to whom the Lord has given the grace of working should do their work faithfully and devotedly so that, avoiding idleness, the enemy of the soul, they do not extinguish the Spirit of holy prayer and devotion to which all other things of our earthly existence must contribute.

also 1R 7:3–12
    Test 20–22

WRITING OF CLARE: RCL 7:1–5

The sisters to whom the Lord has given the grace of working are to work faithfull and devoted, [beginning] after the Hour of Terce, at work which pertains to a virtuous life and to the common good. They must do this in such a way that, while they banish idleness, the enemy of the soul, they do not extinguish the Spirit of holy prayer and devotion to which all other things of our earthly existence must contribute.

And the Abbess or her vicar is bound to assign at the Chapter, in the presence of all, the manual work each is to perform. The same is to be done if alms have been sent by anyone for the needs of the sisters, so that the donors may be remembered by all in prayer together. And all such things are to be distributed for the common good by the Abbess or her vicar with the advice of the discreets.

FRANCISCAN SOURCES: 2CEL 161

Francis used to say that the lukewarm who did not make themselves acquainted familiarly with work would be quickly vomited from the mouth of the Lord. No one could appear idle before him without being corrected by him with a sharp rebuke. For he himself worked and labored with his hands as an example of all perfection, allowing nothing of that greatest gift of time to escape. But he said once: "I want all my brothers to work and to be employed, and those who do not know how should learn some crafts." And he gave this reason: "That we may be less burdensome to men," he said, "and the heart or tongue may not wander to unlawful things in idleness." But the profit of the reward of labor he did not commit to the free disposition of the laborer but to the disposition of the guardian or of the family.

also SP 75

VATICAN II DOCUMENT: GS 34–35

Individual and collective activity, that monumental effort of man through the centuries to improve the circumstances of the world, presents no problem to believers: considered in itself, it corresponds to the plan of God. Man was created in God's image and was commanded to conquer the earth with all it contains and to rule the world in justice and holiness: he was to acknowledge God as maker of all things and relate himself and the totality of creation to him, so that through the dominion of all things by man the name of God would be majestic in all the earth.

This holds good also for our daily work. When men and women provide for themselves and their families in such a way as to be of service to the community as well, they can rightly look upon their work as a prolongation of the work of the creator, a service to their fellow men, and their personal contribution to the fulfillment in history of the divine plan.

Far from considering the conquests of man's genius and courage as opposed to God's power as if he set himself up as a rival to the creator, Christians ought to be convinced that the achievements of the human race are a sign of God's greatness and the fulfillment of his mysterious design. With an increase in human power comes a broadening of responsibility on the part of individuals and communities: there is no question, then, of the Christian message inhibiting men from building up the world or making them disinterested in the good of their fellows: on the contrary it is an incentive to do these very things.

Human activity proceeds from man: it is also ordered to him. When he works, not only does he transform matter and society, but he fulfills himself. He learns, he develops his faculties, and he emerges from and transcends himself. Rightly understood, this kind of growth is more precious than any kind of wealth that can be amassed. It is what man is, rather than what he has, that counts. Technological progress is of less value than advances toward greater justice, wider brotherhood, and a more humane social environment. Technical progress may supply the material for human advancement but it is powerless to actualize it.

Here then is the norm for human activity—to harmonize with the authentic interests of the human race, in accordance with God's will and design, and to enable men as individuals and as members of society to pursue and fulfill their total vocation.

also LG 41e
   AA 13
   GS 67

PAPAL STATEMENT: LE INTRO

Through work man must earn his daily bread and contribute to continual advances of science and technology and, above all, to elevating unceasingly the cultural and moral level of the society within which he lives in community with those who belong to the same family. And work means any activity by man, whether manual or intellectual, whatever its nature or circumstances, it means any human activity that can and must be recognized as work, in the midst of all the many activities of which man is capable and to which he is predisposed by his very nature, by virtue of humanity itself. Man is made to be in the visible universe an image and likeness of God himself, and he is placed in it in order to subdue the earth. From the beginning therefore he is called to work. Work is one of the characteristics that distinguish man from the rest of creatures, whose activity for sustaining their lives cannot be called work. Only man is capable of work, and only man works, at the same time by work occupying his existence on earth. Thus work bears a particular mark of man and of humanity, the mark of a person operating within a community of persons. And this mark decides its interior characteristics, in a sense constitutes its very nature.

also LE 1,4 8, 9, 9b, 16, 25, 25b, 26, 27
  PP 27

PRAYER: FOR THE BLESSING OF MAN'S LABOR

God our Father,
by human labor you govern and guide to perfection
the work of creation.
Hear the prayers of your people
and give to all work that enhances their human dignity
and draws them closer to each other
in the service of their brothers and sisters.
We ask this through Christ our Lord. Amen.

Article 17

In their family they should cultivate the Franciscan spirit of peace, fidelity, and respect for life, striving to make of it a sign of a world already redeemed in Christ.

By living the grace of matrimony, husbands and wives in particular should bear witness in the world to the love of Christ for his Church. They should joyfully accompany their children on their human and spiritual journey by providing a simple and open Christian education and being attentive to the vocation of each child.

THEME: BUILDING THE CHRISTIAN FAMILY AND FULFILLING ITS MISSION

GOSPEL: MK 3:31–36

His mother and brothers now arrived and, standing outside, sent in a message asking for him. A crowd was sitting round him at the time the message was passed to him, "Your mother and brothers and sisters are outside asking for you." He replied, "Who are my mother and my brothers?" And looking round at those sitting in a circle about him, he said, "Here are my mother and my brothers. Anyone who does the will of God, that person is my brother and sister and mother."

NEW TESTAMENT: EPH 5:21–6:14

Give way to one another in obedience to Christ. Wives should regard their husbands as they regard the Lord, since as Christ is head of the Church and saves the whole body, so is a husband the head of his wife, and as the Church submits to Christ, so should wives to their husbands, in everything. Husbands should love their wives just as Christ loved the Church and sacrificed himself for her to make her holy. He made her clean by washing her in water with a form of words, so that when he took her to himself she would be glorious, with no speck or wrinkle or anything like that, but holy and faultless. In the same way, husbands must love their wives as they love their own bodies, for a man to love his wife is for him to love himself. A man never hates his own body, but he feeds it and looks after it, and this is the way Christ treats the Church, because it is his body—and we are its living parts. For this reason, a man must leave his father and mother and be joined to his wife, and the two will become one body. This mystery has many implications, but I am saying it applies to Christ and the Church. To sum up, you too, each one of you, must love his wife as he loves himself, and let every wife respect her husband.

Children, be obedient to your parents in the Lord—that is your duty. The first commandment that has a promise attached to it is: Honor your father and mother, and the promise is: and you will prosper and have a long life in the land. And parents, never drive your children to resentment but in bringing them up correct them and guide them as the Lord does.

OLD TESTAMENT: DEUT 6:4–9

Listen, Israel: Yahweh our God is the one Yahweh. You shall love Yahweh your God with all your heart, with all your soul, with all your strength. Let these words I urge on your today be written on your heart. You shall repeat them to your children and say them over to them whether at rest in your house or walking abroad, at your lying down or at your rising, you shall fasten them on your hand as a sign and on your forehead as a circlet, you shall write them on the doorposts of your house and on your gates.

also Sir 30:1–3

PSALM 128

O blessed are those who fear the Lord
and walk in his ways!

By the labor of your hands you shall eat.
You will be happy and prosper,
your wife like a fruitful vine
in the heart of your house,
your children like shoots of the olive,
around your table.
Indeed thus shall be blessed

the man who fears the Lord.
May the Lord bless you from Zion
all the days of your life!
May you see your children's children
in a happy Jerusalem!

On Israel, peace!

WRITING OF FRANCIS: 2LF 48–53

And upon all men and women, if they have done these things and persevered to the end, the Spirit of the Lord will rest and He will make His home and dwelling among them. They will be children of the heavenly Father whose works they do. And they are spouses, brothers, and mothers of our Lord Jesus Christ. We are spouses when the faithful soul is joined to Jesus Christ by the Holy Spirit. We are brothers when we do the will of His Father Who is in heaven. (We are) mothers when we carry Him in our heart and body through love and a pure and sincere conscience, we give birth to Him through (His) holy manner of working, which should shine before others as an example.

WRITING OF CLARE: RCL 10:9

Each should make known her needs to the other with confidence. For if a mother loves and nourishes her daughter according to the flesh, how much more lovingly must a sister love and nourish her sister according to the spirit.

FRANCISCAN SOURCES: 2CEL 180

St. Francis, exhorting all moreover to charity, admonished them to show to one another affability and the friendliness of family life. "I wish," he said, "that my brothers would show themselves to be children of the same mother and that if anyone asks for a tunic or a cord or anything else, the other should give it to him with generosity. Let them share their books and anything else that is agreeable, so much so that one would even force the other to take it." And lest in this matter he should speak anything of those things that Christ was not working through him, he was the first to do all these things.

VATICAN II DOCUMENT: AA 11

The Creator of all made the married state the beginning and foundation of human society, by his grace he has made of it too, a great mystery in Christ and in the Church (cf. Eph 5:32), and so the apostolate of married persons and of families has a special importance for both Church and civic society.

Christian couples are, for each other, for their children and for their relatives, cooperators of graces and witnesses of the faith. They are the first to pass on the faith to their children and to educate them in it. By word and example they form them to a Christian and apostolic life, they offer them wise guidance in the choice of vocation, and if they discover in them a sacred vocation they encourage it with all care.

To give clear proof in their own lives of the indissolubility and holiness of the marriage bond, to assert with vigor the right and duty of parents and guardians to give their children a Christian upbringing, to defend the dignity and legitimate autonomy of the family: this has always been the duty of married persons; today, however, it has become the most important aspect of their apostolate. They and all the faithful, therefore, should collaborate with men of good will in seeing that these rights are perfectly safeguarded in civil legislation; that in social administration consideration is given to the requirements of families in the matter of housing, education of children, working conditions, social security and taxes; and that in emigration regulations family life is perfectly safeguarded.

The mission of being the primary cell of society has been given to the family by God himself. This mission will be accomplished if the family, by the mutual affection of its members and by family prayer, presents itself as a domestic sanctuary of the Church; if the whole family takes its part in the Church's liturgical worship; if, finally, it offers active hospitality, and practices justice and other good works for the benefit of all its brothers suffering from want. Among the various works of the family apostolate the following may be listed: adopting abandoned children, showing a loving welcome to strangers, helping with the running of schools, supporting adolescents with advice and help, assisting engaged couples to make a better preparation for marriage, taking a share in catechism-teaching, supporting married people and families in a material and moral crisis, and in the case of the aged not only providing them with what is indispensable but also procuring for them a fair share of the fruits of economic progress.

Everywhere and always, but especially in regions where the first seeds of the Gospel are just bring sown, or where the Church is still in its infancy or finds itself in a critical situation, Christian families bear a very valuable witness to Christ before the world when all their life they remain attached to the Gospel and hold up the example of Christian marriage.

To attain the ends of their apostolate more easily it can be of advantage for families to organize themselves into groups.

also LG 11, 35c, 41e
    GS 48

PAPAL STATEMENT: JP, P. 21

The Christian family is so important, and its role is so basic in transforming the world and in building up the kingdom of God, that the council called it a "domestic church" (LG 11). Let us never grow tired of proclaiming the family as a community of love: conjugal love unites the couple and is procreative of new life. It mirrors divine love, is communicated and, in the words of "Gaudium et Spes," is actually a sharing in the covenant of love of Christ and his church (48).

We were all given the great gift of being born into such a community of love: it will be easy for us to uphold its value. And then we must encourage parents in their role as educators of their children—the first catechists and the best ones. What a great task and challenge they have: to teach children the love of God, to make it something real for them. And by God's grace, how easily some families can fulfill the role of being a "primum seminarium" (*Optatam Totius 2*): the germ of a vocation to the priesthood is nourished through family prayer, the example of faith and the support of love.

What a wonderful thing it is when families realize the power they have for the sanctification of the world: the mutual sanctification of husband and wife and the reciprocal influence between parents and children.

And then, by the loving witness of their lives families can bring

Christ's Gospel to others. A vivid realization of the sharing of the laity—and especially the family—in the salvific mission of the church is one of the greatest legacies of the Second Vatican Council. We can never thank God enough for this gift. It is up to us to keep this realization strong, by supporting and defending the family— each and every family....

The holiness of the Christian family is indeed a most apt means for producing the serene renewal of the church which the council so eagerly desired. Through family prayer, the "ecclesia domestica" becomes an effective reality and leads to the transformation of the world.

And all the efforts of parents to instill God's love into their children and to support them by the example of faith, constitute a most relevant apostolate for the twentieth century. Parents with special problems are worthy of our particular pastoral care and all our love.

Dear brothers, we want you to know where our priorities lie. Let us do everything we can for the Christian family, so that our people may fulfill their great vocation in Christian joy and share intimately and effectively in the church's mission—Christ's mission—of salvation.

(John Paul I, Address to Group of Visiting U.S. Bishops,
Sept. 21, 1978)

also FC 27 17, 36, 43, 49
      EN 71

PRAYER ADAPTED FROM NUPTIAL BLESSING B

Father,
to reveal the plan of your love,
you made the union of husband and wife
an image of the covenant between you and your people.
In the fulfillment of this sacrament,
the marriage of Christian man and woman
is a sign of the marriage between Christ and the Church.
Father, stretch out your hand and bless all married couples.
Grant that they may share with each other the gifts of
        your love
and become one in heart and mind

as witnesses to your presence in their marriage.
Help them to create a home together.
May their children be formed by the gospel
and have a place in your family.
We ask this through Christ our Lord. Amen.

Article 18

Moreover they should respect all creatures, animate and inanimate, which "bear the imprint of the Most High," and they should strive to move from the temptation of exploiting creations to the Franciscan concept of universal kinship.

THEME: ESTABLISHING THE PROPER RELATIONSHIP WITH CREATION

GOSPEL: LK 21:29–33

And he told them a parable, "Think of the fig tree and indeed every tree. As soon as you see them bud, you know that summer is now near. So with you when you see these things happening: know that the kingdom of God is near. I tell you solemnly, before this generation has passed away all will have taken place. Heaven and earth will pass away, but my words will never pass away."

NEW TESTAMENT: REV 21:1–6

Then I saw a new heaven and a new earth, the first heaven and the first earth had disappeared now, and there was no longer any sea. I saw the holy city, and the new Jerusalem, coming down from God out of heaven, as beautiful as a bride all dressed for her husband. Then I heard a loud voice call from the throne, "You see this city? Here God lives among men. He will make his home among them; they shall be his people, and he will be their God, his name is God-with-them. He will wipe away all tears from their eyes, there will be no more death, and no more mourning or sadness. This world of the past has gone."

The One sitting on the throne spoke: "Now I am making the whole of creation new," he said. "Write this: that what I am saying is sure and will come true." And then he said, "It is already done. I am the Alpha and the Omega, the Beginning and the End."

OLD TESTAMENT: SIR 42:15–43:35

I will remind you of the works of the Lord,
and tell of what I have seen.
By the words of the Lord his works come into being
and all creation obeys his will.
As the sun in shining looks on all things,
so the work of the Lord is full of his glory.
The Lord has not granted to the holy ones
to tell of his marvels
which the Almighty Lord has solidly constructed
for the universe to stand firm in his glory.
He has fathomed the deep and the heart,
and seen into their devious ways,
for the Most High knows all the knowledge there is,
and has observed the signs of the times.
He declares what is past and what will be,
and uncovers the traces of hidden things.
Not a thought escapes him,
not a single word is hidden from him.
He has imposed an order on the magnificent words
        his wisdom:
he is from everlasting to everlasting,
nothing can be added to him, nothing taken away,
he needs no one's advice.
How desirable are all his works,
how dazzling to the eye!
They all live and last forever,
whatever the circumstances all obey him.
All things go in pairs, by opposites,
and he has made nothing defective,
the one consolidates the excellence of the other,
who could ever be sated with gazing at his glory?
Pride of the heights, shining vault,
so, in a glorious spectacle, the sky appears.
The sun, as he emerges, proclaims at his rising,
A thing of wonder is the work of the Most High!
At his zenith he parches the land,
who can withstand his blaze?
A man must blow a furnace to produce any heat,

the sun burns the mountains three times as much,
breathing out blasts of fire,
flashing his rays he dazzles the eyes.
Great is the Lord who made him,
and whose word speeds him on his course.
And then the moon, always punctual, to mark
        the months and make division of time:
the moon it is that signals the feasts, a luminary
        that wanes after her full.
The month derives its name from hers,
        she waxes wonderfully in her phases,
banner of the hosts on high, shining in the vault of heaven.
The glory of the stars makes the beauty of the sky,
        a brilliant decoration to the heights of the Lord.
At the words of the Holy One they stand as he decrees,
        and never grow slack at their watch.
See the rainbow and praise its maker, so superbly
        beautiful in its splendor.
Across the sky it forms a glorious arc drawn by
        the hands of the Most High.
By his command he sends the snow, he speeds
        the lightning as he orders.
In the same way, his treasuries open and
        the clouds fly out like birds.
In his great might he banks up the clouds,
        and shivers them into fragments of hail.
At sight of him the mountains rock, at the roar
        of his thunder the earth writhes in labor.
At his will the south wind blows, or the storm
        from the north and the whirlwind.
He sprinkles snow like birds alighting, it comes
        down like locusts settling.
The eye marvels at the beauty of its whiteness,
        and the mind is amazed at its falling.
Over the earth, like salt, he also pours hoarfrost, which,
        when it freezes, bristles like thorns.
The cold wind blows from the north, and ice forms
        on the water,
settling on every watery expanse, and water puts it on
        like a breastplate.

He swallows up the mountains and scorches the desert,
    like a fire he consumes the vegetation.
But the mist heals everything in good time,
    after the heat falls the reviving dew.
By his own resourcefulness he has tamed the abyss,
    and planted it with islands.
Those who sail the sea tell of its dangers, their accounts
    fill our ears with amazement:
for there too there are strange and wonderful works,
    animals of every kind and huge sea creatures.
Thanks to him all ends well, and all things hold together
    by means of his word.
We could say much more and still fall short,
    to put it concisely, He is all.
Where shall we find sufficient power to glorify him,
    since he is the Great One, above all his works,
the awe-inspiring Lord, stupendously great,
    and wonderful in his power?
Exalt the Lord in your praises as high as you may—
    still he surpasses you.
Exert all your strength when you exalt him,
    do not grow tired—you will never come to the end.
Who has ever seen him to give a description?
    Who can glorify him as he deserves?
Many mysteries remain even greater than these,
    for we have seen only a few of his works,
the Lord himself having made all things—
    and having given wisdom to devout men.

also Dan 3:57–90

PSALM 19A

The heavens proclaim the glory of God
and the firmament shows forth the work of his hands.
Day unto day takes up the story
and night unto night makes known the message.

No speech, no word, no voice is heard
yet their span extends through all the earth,

their words to the utmost bounds of the world.

There he has placed a tent for the sun,
it comes forth like a bridegroom coming from his tent,
rejoices like a champion to run its course.

At the end of the sky is the rising of the sun,
to the furthest end of the sky is its course.
There is nothing concealed from its burning heat.

WRITING OF FRANCIS: CANTSUN

Most High, all-powerful, good Lord,
Yours are the praises, the glory, the honor, and all blessing.
To You alone, Most High, do they belong,
and no man is worthy to mention Your name.
Praised be You, my Lord, with all your creatures,
especially Sir Brother Son,
Who is the day and through whom You give us light.
And he is beautiful and radiant with great splendor,
and bears a likeness of You, Most High One.
Praised be You, my Lord, through Sister moon
            and the stars,
in heaven You formed them clear and precious
            and beautiful.
Praised be You, my Lord, through Brother Wind,
and through the air, cloudy and serene,
            and every kind of weather
through which You give sustenance to Your creatures.
Praised be You, my Lord, through Sister Water,
which is very useful and humble and precious and chaste.
Praised be You, my Lord, through Brother Fire,
through whom You light the night
and he is beautiful and playful and robust and strong.
Praised be You, my Lord, through our Sister Mother Earth,
who sustains and governs us,
and who produces varied fruits with colored flowers
            and herbs.
Praised be You, my Lord, through those who give pardon
            for Your love

and bear infirmity and tribulation.
Blessed are those who endure in peace
for by You, Most High, they shall be crowned.
Praised be You, my Lord, through our Sister Bodily Death,
from whom no living man can escape.
Woe to those who die in mortal sin.
Blessed are those whom death will find in
    Your most holy will,
for the second death shall do them no harm.
Praise and bless my Lord and give Him thanks
and serve Him with great humility.

WRITING OF CLARE: 3L 13–17,22–23

Since you have cast aside all [those] things which, in this deceitful and turbulent world, ensnare their blind lovers, love Him totally Who gave Himself totally for Your love. His beauty the sun and moon admire; and of his gifts there is no limit in abundance, preciousness, and magnitude. I am speaking of Him Who is the Son of the Most High, Whom the Virgin brought to birth and remained a virgin after His birth.... For the heavens with the rest of creation cannot contain their Creator. Only the faithful soul through the charity which the wicked do not have. [He Who is] the Truth has said: Whoever loves me will be loved by My Father, and I too shall love him, and We shall come to him and make our dwelling place with Him (Jn 14:21).

FRANCISCAN SOURCES: 2CEL 165

Hurrying to leave this world in as much as it is the place of exile of our pilgrimage, this blessed traveler was yet helped not a little by the things that are in the world. With respect to the world-rulers of this darkness, he used it as a field of battle, with respect to God, he used it as a very bright image of his goodness. In every work of the artist he praised the Artist, whatever he found in the things made he referred to the Maker. He rejoiced in all the works of the hands of the Lord and saw behind things pleasant to behold their life-giving reason and cause. In beautiful things he saw Beauty itself, all things were to him good. "He who made us is the best," they cried out to him. Through his footprints impressed upon things he followed the

Beloved everywhere, he made for himself from all things a ladder by which to come even to his throne.

He embraced all things with a rapture of unheard of devotion, speaking to them of the Lord and admonishing them to praise him. He spared lights, lamps, and candles, not wishing to extinguish their brightness with his hand, for he regarded them as a symbol of Eternal Light. He walked reverently upon stones, because of him who was called the Rock. When he used this versicle: Thou has exalted me on a rock, he would say for the sake of greater reverence: Thou hast exalted me at the foot of a rock.

He forbade the brothers to cut down the whole tree when they cut wood, so that it might have hope of sprouting again. He commanded the gardener to leave the border around the garden undug, so that in their proper times the greenness of grass and the beauty of flowers might announce the beauty of the Father in all things. He commanded that a little place be set aside in the garden for sweet-smelling and flowering plants, so that they would bring those who look upon them to the memory of the Eternal Sweetness.

He removed from the road little worms, lest they be crushed under foot, and he ordered that honey and the best wines be set out for the bees, lest they perish from want in the cold of winter. He called all animals by the name brother, though among all the kinds of animals he preferred the gentle. Who could possibly narrate everything? For that original goodness that will be one day all things in all already shown forth in this saint all things in all.

also SP 113

VATICAN II DOCUMENT: LG 36B

The faithful must recognize the inner nature, the value and the ordering of the whole of creation to the praise of God. Even by their secular activity they must aid one another to greater holiness of life, so that the world may be filled with the spirit of Christ and may the more effectively attain its destiny in justice, in love and in peace. The laity enjoy a principle role in the universal fulfillment of this task. Therefore, by their competence in secular disciplines and by their activity, interiorly raised up by grace, let them work earnestly in order that created goods through human labor, technical skill, and civil culture may serve the utility of all men according to the plan of the creator and the light of his word. May these goods be more suitably distributed among all men and in their own way may they be conducive to universal progress in human and Christian liberty. Thus, through the members of the Church, will Christ increasingly illuminate the whole of human society with his saving light.

also GS 37

PAPAL STATEMENT: PP 27

Created according to the image of God, "man must cooperate with the Creator to perfect the work of creation and must in turn place upon the earth the spiritual image stamped upon himself." When God endowed man with intellect, power to reason, and sensitivity he gave him the means with which to complete and perfect, as it were, the work begun by Himself, for whoever engages in work, be he artist, artisan, manager, laborer, farmer, in a certain sense creates. As he struggles with materials which resist his efforts man, as it were, leaves some imprint of himself upon them while at the same time refining his persistency, skill, and power to think. Furthermore, since work which men share together causes them to have common hopes, sorrows, desires, and joys it unites their wills, their minds, and hearts. For when men work they recognize one another as brothers.

also LB 25

PRAYER: SEVENTEENTH SUNDAY IN ORDINARY TIME

God our Father,
open our eyes to see your hand at work
in the splendor of creation,
in the beauty of human life.
Touched by your hand our world is holy.
Help us to cherish the gifts that surround us,
to share your blessings with our brothers and sisters:
and to experience the joy of life in your presence.
We ask this through Christ our Lord. Amen.

Article 19

Mindful that they are bearers of peace which must be built up unceasingly, they should seek out ways of unity and fraternal harmony through dialogue, trusting in the presence of the divine seed in everyone and in the transforming power of love and pardon.

Messengers of perfect joy in every circumstance, they should strive to bring joy and hope to others.

Since they are immersed in the resurrection of Christ, which gives true meaning to Sister Death, let them serenely tend toward the ultimate encounter with the Father.

Theme: Becoming a Peace-maker in all Circumstances

Gospel: Jn 14:27–31

Peace I bequeath to you,
my own peace I give you,
a peace the world cannot give, this is my gift to you.
Do not let your hearts be troubled or afraid.
You heard me say:
I am going away, and shall return.
If you loved me you would have been glad to know
       that I am going to the Father,
for the Father is greater than I.
I have told you this now before it happens,
so that when it does happen you may believe.
I shall not talk with you any longer,
because the prince of this world is on his way.
He has no power over me,
but the world must be brought to know
       that I love the Father
and that I am doing exactly what the Father told me.

New Testament: Eph 4:1–6

I, the prisoner in the Lord, implore you therefore to lead a life worthy of your vocation. Bear with one another charitably, in com-

plete selflessness, gentleness and patience. Do all you can to preserve
the unity of the Spirit by the peace that binds you together. There is
one Body, one Spirit, just as you were all called into one and the
same hope when you were called. There is one Lord, one faith, one
baptism, and one God who is Father of all, over all, through all and
within all.

OLD TESTAMENT: IS 2:2–5

In the days to come
the mountain of the Temple of Yahweh
shall tower above the mountains
and be lifted higher than the hills.
All the nations will stream to it,
peoples without number will come to it, and they will say:
"Come, let us go up to the mountain of Yahweh,
to the Temple of the God of Jacob
that he may teach us his ways
so that we may walk in his paths,
since the Law will go out from Zion,
and the oracle of Yahweh from Jerusalem."
He will wield authority over the nations
and adjudicate between many peoples,
these will hammer their swords into ploughshares,
their spears into sickles.
Nation will not lift sword against nation,
there will be no more training for war.
O House of Jacob, come,
let us walk in the light of Yahweh.

also Is 32:15–20
    Is 57:15–19

PSALM 85

O Lord, you once favored your land
and revived the fortunes of Jacob,
you forgave the guilt of your people
and covered all their sins.
You averted all your rage,

you calmed the heat of your anger.

Revive us now, God, our helper!
Put an end to your grievance against us.
Will you be angry with us for ever,
will your anger never cease?

Will you not restore again our life
that your people may rejoice in you?
Let us see, O Lord, your mercy
and give us your saving help.

I will hear what the Lord has to say,
a voice that speaks of peace,
peace for his people and his friends
and those who turn to him in their hearts.
His help is near for those who fear him
and his glory will dwell in our land.
Mercy and faithfulness have met,
justice and peace have embraced.
Faithfulness shall spring from the earth
and justice look down from heaven.

The Lord will make us prosper
and our earth shall yield its fruit.
Justice shall march before him
and peace shall follow his steps.

WRITING OF FRANCIS: ADM 15

"Blessed are the peacemakers, for they shall be called the children of God." The true peacemakers are those who preserve peace of mind and body for love of our Lord Jesus Christ, despite what they suffer in this world.

also Test 23

WRITING OF CLARE: 4L 14–32

Inasmuch as this vision is the spendor of eternal glory (Heb 1:3), the brilliance of eternal ight and the mirror without blemish (Wis

7:26), look upon that mirror each day, O queen and spouse of Jesus Christ, and continually study your face within it, so that you may adorn yourself within and without with beautiful robes and cover yourself with the flowers and garments of all the virtues, as becomes the daughter and most chaste bride of the Most High King. Indeed, blessed poverty, holy humility, and ineffable charity are reflected in that mirror, as, with the grace of God, you can contemplate them throughout the entire mirror.

Look at the parameters of this mirror, that is, the poverty of Him Who was placed in a manger and wrapped in swaddling clothes. O marvelous humility, O astonishing poverty! The King of the angels, the Lord of heaven and earth, is laid in a manger! Then, at the surface of the mirror, dwell on the holy humility, the blessed poverty, the untold labors and burdens which He endured for the redemption of all mankind. Then, in the depths of this same mirror, contemplate the ineffable charity which led Him to suffer on the wood of the Cross and die thereupon the most shameful kind of death. Therefore, that Mirror, suspended on the wood of the Cross, urged those who passed by to consider, saying "All you who pass by the way, look and see if there is any suffering like My suffering!" (Lam 1:12). Let us answer Him with one voice and spirit, as He said: Remembering this over and over leaves my soul downcast within me! (Lam 3:20) From this moment, then, O queen of our heavenly King, let yourself be inflamed more strongly with the fervor of charity!

[As you] contemplate further His ineffable delights, eternal riches and honors, and sigh for them in the great desire and love of your heart, may you cry out:

> Draw me after You!
> We will run in the fragrance of Your perfumes,
>   O heavenly Spouse!
> I will run and not tire,
>   until You bring me into the wine-cellar,
>   until You left hand is under my head
>   and Your right hand will embrace me happily
>   [and] You will kiss me with the happiest kiss of
>   Your mouth (Cant 1:1,3; 2:4,6).

FRANCISCAN SOURCES: 3SOC 58

Francis also said to the brothers: "Since you speak of peace, all the more so must you have it in your hearts. Let none be provoked to anger or scandal by you, but rather may they be drawn to peace and good will, to benignity and concord through your gentleness. We have been called to heal wounds, to unite what has fallen apart, and to bring home those who have lost their way. Many who may seem to us to be children of the Devil will still become Christ's disciples."

also lCel 23, 29
    3Soc 26, 29

VATICAN II DOCUMENT: GS 78

Peace is more than the absence of war: it cannot be reduced to the maintenance of a balance of power between opposing forces nor does it arise out of despotic dominion, but it is appropriately called "the effect of righteousness" (Is 32:17). It is the fruit of that right ordering of things with which the divine founder has invested human society and which must be actualized by man thirsting after an ever more perfect reign of justice. But while the common good of mankind ultimately derives from the eternal law, it depends in the concrete upon circumstances which change as time goes on, consequently, peace will never be achieved once and for all, but must be built up continually. Since, moreover, human nature is weak and wounded by sin, the achievement of peace requires a constant effort to control the passions and unceasing vigilance by lawful authority.

But this is not enough. Peace cannot be obtained on earth unless the welfare of man is safeguarded and people freely and trustingly share with one another the riches of their minds and their talents. A firm determination to respect the dignity of other men and other peoples along with the deliberate practice of fraternal love are absolutely necessary for the achievement of peace. Accordingly, peace is also the fruit of love, for love goes beyond what justice can ensure.

Peace on earth, which flows from love of one's neighbor, symbolizes and derives from the peace of Christ who proceeds from God the Father. Christ, the Word made flesh, the prince of peace, reconciled all men to God by the cross, and, restoring the unity of all in one people and one body, he abolished hatred in his own flesh, having been lifted up through his resurrection, he poured forth the Spirit of love into the hearts of men. Therefore, all Christians are earnestly to speak the truth in love (cf. Eph 4:35) and join with all peace-loving men in pleading for peace and trying to bring it about. In the same spirit we cannot but express our admiration for all who forgo the use of violence to vindicate their rights and resort to those other means of defense which are available to weaker parties, provided it can be done without harm to the rights and duties of others and of the community. Insofar as men are sinners, the threat of war hangs over them and will continue until the coming of Christ, but insofar as they can vanquish sin by coming together in charity, violence itself will be vanquished and they will make these words come true: "They shall beat their swords into ploughshares, their spears into pruning hooks, nations shall not lift up the sword against nations, neither shall they learn war any more" (Is 2:4).

also LG 51

PAPAL STATEMENT: PT 1,165,167–8

Peace on earth, which all men of every era have most eagerly yearned for, can be firmly established only if the order laid down by God is dutifully observed...

There can be no peace between men unless there is peace within each one of them, unless, that is, each one builds up within himself the order wished by God....

Peace will be but an empty-sounding word unless it is founded on the order which this present document has outlined in confident hope: an order founded on truth, built according to justice, vivified and integrated by charity, and put into practice in freedom. This is such a noble and elevated task that human resources, even though inspired by the most praiseworthy good will, cannot bring it to realization alone. In order that human society may reflect as faithfully as possible the Kingdom of God, help from on high is absolutely necessary.

also PP 76

PRAYER:

Lord, make me an instrument of your peace
Where there is hatred, let me sow love.
Where there is injury, pardon.
Where there is doubt, faith.
Where there is despair, hope.
Where there is darkness, light.
Where there is sadness, joy.
O Divine Master,
grant that I may not so much seek
to be consoled, as to console,
to be understood, as to understand,
to be loved, as to love.
For it is in giving that we receive,
it is in pardoning that we are pardoned.
And it is in dying that we are born
to eternal life. Amen.

(FOR PEACE AND JUSTICE)

Lord,
you guide all creation with fatherly care.
As you have given all people one common origin,
bring them peacefully into one family
and keep them united in brotherly love.
We ask this through Christ our Lord. Amen.

chapter three

Life in Fraternity

T Article 20

The Secular Franciscan Order is divided into fraternities of levels—local, regional, national, and international. Each various levels—local, regional, national, and international—each one has its own moral personality in the Church. These various fraternities are coordinated and united according to the norm of this rule and of the constitutions.

THEME: FRATERNITY AS CONTEXT FOR
FAITHFUL GOSPEL LIVING

GOSPEL: JN 17:21–26

> May they all be one.
> Father, may they be one in us,
> as you are in me and I am in you,
> so that the world may believe it was you who sent me.
> I have given them the glory you gave to me,
> that they may be one as we are one.
> With me in them and you in me,
> may they be so completely one

that the world will realize that it was you who sent me
and that I have loved them as much as you loved me.
Father,
I want those you have given me
to be with me where I am,
so that they may always see the glory
you have given me
because you loved me
before the foundation of the world.
Father, Righteous One,
the world has not know you,
but I have known you,
and these have known
that you sent me.
I have made your name known to them
and will continue to make it known,
so that the love with which you loved me may be in them,
so that I may be in them.

NEW TESTAMENT: ROM 12:4–11

Just as each of our bodies has several parts and each part has a separate function, so all of us, in union with Christ, form one body, and as parts of it we belong to each other. Our gifts differ according to the grace given us. If your gift is prophecy, then use it as your faith suggests; if administration, then use it for administration; if teaching, then use it for teaching. Let the preachers deliver sermons, the almsgivers give freely, the officials be diligent, and those who do works of mercy do them cheerfully.

Do not let your love be a pretense, but sincerely prefer good to evil. Love each other as much as brothers should, and have a profound respect for each other. Work for the Lord with untiring effort and with great earnestness of spirit.

also 1 Car 12:12–30

OLD TESTAMENT: EZ 37:21–22,26–28

The Lord Yahweh says this: I am going to take the sons of Israel from the nations where they have gone. I shall gather them together from everywhere and bring them home to their own soil. I shall make them one nation in my own land and on the mountain of Israel, and one king is to be king of them all, they will no longer form two nations, nor be two separate kingdoms.... I shall make a covenant of peace with them, an eternal covenant with them. I shall resettle them and increase them, I shall settle my sanctuary among them for ever. I shall make my home above them, I will be their God, they shall be my people. And the nations will learn that I am Yahweh the sanctifier of Israel, when my sanctuary is with them for ever.

also Jer 32:37–41

PSALM 133

How good and how pleasant it is
when brothers live in unity!

It is like precious oil upon the head
running down the beard,
running down upon Aaron's beard,
upon the collar of his robes.

It is like the dew of Hermon which falls
on the heights of Zion.
For there the Lord gives his blessing:
life for ever.

WRITING OF FRANCIS: 2R 6:7–9

And wherever the brothers may be together and meet (other) brothers, let them give witness that they are members of one family. And let each one confidently make known his need to the other, for, if a mother has such care and love for her son born according to the flesh, should not someone love and care for his brothers according to the Spirit even more diligently? And if any of them becomes sick, the other brothers should serve him as they would wish to be served themselves.

also 1R 7:15–16

WRITING OF CLARE: RCL 10:4–5

I admonish and exhort in the Lord Jesus Christ that the sisters be on their guard against all pride, vainglory, envy, greed, worldly care and anxiety, detraction and murmuring, dissension and division. Let them be ever zealous to preserve among themselves the unity of mutual love, which is the bond of perfection.

FRANCISCAN SOURCES: 2 CEL 191–2

It was always Francis' anxious wish and careful watchfulness to preserve among his sons the bond of unity, so that those whom the same spirit drew together and the same father brought forth might be nurtured peacefully in the bosom of one mother. He wanted the greater to be joined to the lesser, the wise to be united with the simple by brotherly affection, the distant to be bound to the distant by the binding force of love. He once set before them (a) moral similitude... (which he) explained in this way. "Our order," he said, "is a very great company, a kind of general assembly, which has come from every part of the world to live under one form of life. In it the wise turn to their advantage what is characteristic of the simple, when they see the illiterate seeking heavenly things with burning zeal and those who have not been taught by men learning to savor spiritual things through the Holy Spirit. In it also the simple turn to their own benefit the things that are proper to the wise, when they see renowned men who could live in glory everywhere in the world humbled in the same way as they themselves. This," he said, "is what makes the beauty of this family shine forth, whose many different ornaments please the father of the family not a little."

VATICAN II DOCUMENT: GS 32

Just as God did not create men to live as individuals but to come together in the formation of social unity, so he "willed to make men holy and save them, not as individuals without any bond or link between them, but rather to make them into a people who might acknowledge him and serve him in holiness." At the outset of salvation history he chose certain men as members of a given community, not as individuals, and revealed his plan to them, calling them "his people" (Ex 3:7–12) and making a covenant on Mount Sinai with them.

This communitarian character is perfected and fulfilled in the work of Jesus Christ, for the Word made flesh willed to share in human fellowship. He was present at the wedding feast at Cana, he visited the house of Zacchaeus, he sat down with publicans and sinners. In revealing the Father's love and man's sublime calling, he made use of the most ordinary things of social life and illustrated his words with expressions and imagery from everyday life. He sanctified those human ties, above all family ties, which are the basis of social structures. He willingly observed the laws of his country and chose to lead the life of an ordinary craftsman of his time and place. In his preaching he clearly outlined an obligation on the part of the sons of God to treat each other as brothers. In his prayer he asked that all his followers should be "one." As the redeemer of all mankind he delivered himself even unto death for the sake of all: "Greater love has no man than this, that a man lay down his life for his friends" (Jn 15:13). His command to the apostles was to preach the Gospel to all peoples in order that the human race would become the family of God, in which love would be the fullness of the law.

As the firstborn of many brethren, and by the gift of his Spirit, he established, after his death and resurrection, a new brotherly communion among all who received him in faith and love; this is the communion of his own body, the Church, in which everyone as members one of the other would render mutual service in the measure of the different gifts bestowed on each.

This solidarity must be constantly increased until that day when it will be brought to fulfillment, on that day mankind, saved by grace, will offer perfect glory to God as the family beloved of God and of Christ their brother.

also LG 9

PAPAL STATEMENT: EN 58c

In some regions "communautes de base" appear and develop, almost without exception, within the Church, having solidarity with her life, being nourished by her teaching and united with her pastors. In these cases, they spring from the need to live the Church's life more intensely, or from the desire and quest for a more human dimension such as larger ecclesial communities can only offer with difficulty, especially in the big modern cities which lend themselves but to life in the mass and to anonymity. Such communities can quite simply be in their own way an extension on the spiritual and religious level—worship, deepening of faith, fraternal charity, prayer, contact with pastors—of the small sociological community such as the village, etc. Or again their aim may be to bring together, for the purpose of listening to and meditating on the Word, for the sacraments and the bond of the "agape," groups of people who are linked by age, culture, civil state or social situation: married couples, young people, professional people, etc., people who already happen to be united in the struggle for justice, brotherly aid to the poor, human advancement. In still other cases they bring Christians together in places where the shortage of priests does not favor the normal life of a parish community. This is all presupposed within communities constituted by the Church, especially individual Churches and parishes.

PRAYER: FOR PROMOTING HARMONY

> God our Father,
> source of unity and love,
> make your faithful people one in heart and mind
> that your Church may live in harmony,
> be steadfast in its profession of faith,
> and secure in unity.
> We ask this through Christ our Lord. Amen.

Article 21

On various levels, each fraternity is animated and guided by a council and minister (or president) who are elected by the professed according to the constitutions.

Their service, which lasts for a definite period, is marked by a ready and willing spirit and is a duty of responsibility to each member and to the community.

Within themselves the fraternities are structured in different ways according to the norm of the constitutions, according to the various needs of their members and their regions, and under the guidance of their respective council.

THEME: THE SERVICE OF LEADERSHIP IN THE SFO COMMUNITY

GOSPEL: MT 20:25-28

Jesus called them to him and said, "You know that among the pagans the rulers lord it over them, and their great men make their authority felt. This is not to happen among you. No, anyone who wants to be great among you must be your servant, and anyone who wants to be first among you must be your slave, just as the Son of Man came not to be served but to serve, and to give his life as a ransom for many."

also Mk 10:41-45
    Lk 22:25-27

NEW TESTAMENT: 2 COR 4:1-7

Since we have by an act of mercy been entrusted with this work of administration, there is no weakening on our part. On the contrary, we will have none of the reticence of those who are ashamed, no deceitfulness or watering down the word of God, but the way we commend ourselves to every human being with a conscience is by stating the truth openly in the sight of God. If our gospel does not penetrate the veil, then the veil is on those who are not on the way to salvation, the unbelievers whose minds the god of this world has blinded, to stop them seeing the light shed by the Good News of the glory of Christ, who is the image of God. For it is not ourselves that we are preaching, but Christ Jesus as the Lord, and ourselves as your servants for Jesus' sake. It is the same God that said, "Let there be light shining out of darkness," who has shone in our minds to radiate the light of the knowledge of God's glory, the glory on the face of Christ. We are only the earthenware jars that hold this treasure, to make it clear that such an overwhelming power comes from God and not from us.

also Col :25–29

OLD TESTAMENT: NUM 11:16–17, 24–25

Yahweh said to Moses, "Gather seventy of the elders of Israel, men you know to be the people's elders and scribes. Bring them to the Tent of Meeting, and let them stand beside you there. I will come down to speak with you, and I will take some of the spirit which is on you and put it on them. So they will share with you the burden of this nation, and you will no longer have to carry it by yourself."

Moses went out and told the people what Yahweh has said. Then he gathered seventy elders of the people and brought them round the Tent. Yahweh came down in the Cloud. He spoke with him, but took some of the spirit that was on him and put it on the seventy elders. When the spirit came on them they prophesied.

also Deut 1:13–18

PSALM 101 (AVOWAL OF A GOOD RULER)

My song is of mercy and justice,
I sing to you, O Lord.
I will walk in the way of perfection.
O when, Lord, will you come?

I will walk with blameless heart
within my house,
I will not set before my eyes
whatever is base.

I will hate the ways of the crooked,
they shall not be my friends.
The false-hearted must keep far away,
the wicked I disown.

The man who slanders his neighbor in secret
I will bring to silence.
The man of proud looks and haughty heart
I will never endure.

I look to the faithful in the land
that they may dwell with me.
He who walks in the way of perfection
shall be my friend.

No man who practices deceit
shall live within my house.
No man who utters lies shall stand
before my eyes.

Morning after morning I will silence
all the wicked in the land,
uprooting from the Lord's city
all who do evil.

WRITING OF FRANCIS: ADM 4

"I did not come to be served but to serve" (cf. Mt 10:28), says the Lord. Those who are placed over others should glory in such an office only as much as they would were they assigned the task of washing the feet of the brothers. And the more they are upset about their office being taken from them than they would be over the loss of the office of (washing) feet, so much the more do they store up treasures to the peril of their souls (cf. Jn 12:6).

also 2LF 42–22
    1R 4:5

WRITING OF CLARE: TCL

I also beg that sister who will have the office [of caring for] the sisters to strive to exceed others more by her virtues and holy life than by her office so that, encouraged by her example, the Sisters may obey her not so much out of duty but rather out of love. Let her also be prudent and attentive to her sisters just as a good mother is to her daughters; and especially, let her take care to provide for them according to the needs of each one from the things which the Lord shall give. Let her also be so kind and so available that all [of them] may reveal their needs with trust and have recourse to her at any hour with confidence as they see fit, both for her sake and that of her sisters.

also RCl 4:7, 10:1–3

FRANCISCAN SOURCES: 2CEL 184–6

Near the end of Francis' vocation in the Lord, a certain brother who was always solicitous for the things of God and filled with love for the order, made this request of Francis: "Father, you will pass away and the family that has followed you will be left abandoned in this valley of tears. Point out someone, if you know of anyone in the order, upon whom your spirit may rest and upon whom the burden of minister general may be safely placed." St. Francis answered, accompanying all his words with sighs: "I see no one, son, who would be capable of being the leader of an army of so many different men and the shepherd of so large a flock. But I would like to describe one for you and fashion one, as the saying goes, with my hand, one in whom it may be clearly seen what kind of man the father of this family must be.

"He must be a man of most serious life," he said, "of great discretion, of praiseworthy reputation. A man who has no private loves, lest while he shows favor to the one, he beget scandal in the whole group. A man to whom zeal for prayer is a close friend, a man who sets aside certain hours for his soul and certain hours for the flock committed to him. For the first thing in the morning he must begin with the holy sacrifice of the Mass and commend himself and his flock to the divine protection in a prolonged devotion. After his prayers," he said, "he should make himself available to be stormed by all, to give answers to all, to provide for all with kindness. He must be a man who will not commit the foul sin of showing favoritism, a man in whom the care of the lowly and the simple is no less pronounced than his care for the wise and the greater. A man who, though it be his gift to excel in learning, bars this image of pious simplicity in his actions and fosters virtue.... He should be a man who consoles the afflicted, since he is the last recourse for the troubled; and if they can find no healing remedies from him, there is danger that the illness of despair may prevail over the sick. He should bend stormy characters to meekness, he should debase himself and relax something of what is his right to gain a soul for Christ. Toward those who take flight from the order let him not shut up the bowels of his mercy, as if they were sheep who had perished, knowing that the temptations that bring a man to such a pass are overpowering temptations.

"I would want him to be honored by all as taking the place of Christ and to be provided with everything that is necessary in all charity. However, he must not take pleasure in honors, nor be pleased by favors more than by injuries. If some time he should need more abundant food because he has grown weak or is exhausted, he should take it not in private but in public, so that others may be spared shame in providing for the weakness of their bodies. Above all else it pertains to him to examine the secrets of conscience, to bring out the truth from hidden places, but not to listen to the talkative. He must be, finally, a man who in no way will bring down the strong fabric of justice by his eagerness for retaining honors, but who will consider so great an office a burden rather than a dignity. However, he should not let apathy grow out of excessive kindness, not a letdown in discipline out of lax indulgence, so that while he is loved by all, he will be none the less feared by those that work evil. I would wish, however, that he have companions endowed with goodness of life who will show themselves, just as he does, in all things an example of good works: men who are staunch against pleasures, strong against hardships, and so becomingly affable that all who come to them may be received with holy cheerfulness. Behold," he said, "this is what the minister general of the order must be."

also 2 Cel 187

VATICAN II DOCUMENT: AA 22

Worthy of special respect and praise in the Church are the laity, single or married, who, in a definitive way or for a period, put their person and their professional competence at the service of institutions and their activities. It is a great joy to the Church to see growing day by day the number of lay people who are offering their personal service to associations and works of the apostolate, whether within the confines of their own country, or in the international field, or, above all, in the Catholic communities of the missions and of the young Churches.

PAPAL STATEMENT: SF 4

And now for those who have specific responsibilities in the Secular Franciscan Order, I hope for a unity of purpose and a sharpened willingness, so that they can be animators and enlightened guides leading the brothers and sisters in love of the Gospel and fidelity to the Church. I thank you for all that you have done up till now in behalf of this same fraternity.

(John Paul II, Exhortation to the SFO Assembly and Congress,
Sept. 27, 1982.)

PRAYER: FOR A COUNCIL OR SYNOD

God our Father,
you judge your people with kindness
and rule us with love.
Give a spirit of wisdom
to those you have entrusted with authority
in your Church
that your people may come to know the truth more fully
and grow in holiness.
Grant this through Christ our Lord. Amen.

Article 22

The local fraternity is to be established canonically. It becomes the basic unit of the whole Order and a visible sign of the Church, a community of love. This should be the privileged place for developing a sense of Church and the Franciscan vocation and for enlivening the apostolic life of its members.

THEME: THE FUNCTION OF FRATERNITY

GOSPEL: JN 14:23–26

> Jesus replied:
> "If anyone loves me he will keep my word,
> and my Father will love him,
> and we shall come to him
> and make our home with him.
> Those who do not love me do not keep my words.
> And my word is not my own:
> it is the word of the one who sent me.
> I have said these things to you
> while still with you,
> but the Advocate, the Holy Spirit,
> whom the Father will send in my name,
> will teach you everything
> and remind you of all that I have said to you."

also Jn 14:1–4

NEW TESTAMENT: PHIL 2:1–5

If our life in Christ means anything to you, if love can persuade at all, or the Spirit that we have in common, or any tenderness and sympathy, then be united in your convictions and united in your love, with a common purpose and a common mind. That is the one thing which would make me completely happy. There must be no competition among you, no conceit, but everybody is to be self-effacing. Always consider the other person to be better than yourself, so that nobody thinks of his own interest first but everybody thinks of other people's interests instead. In your minds you must be same as Christ Jesus.

also Rom 15:5–7,13
        1 Pet 2:9–10

OLD TESTAMENT: 2 CHR 7:11–12, 15–16

Solomon finished the Temple of Yahweh and the royal palace and successfully concluded all he had set his heart on doing in the house of Yahweh and in his own. Then Yahweh appeared to Solomon in the night and said, "I grant your prayer. I choose this place for myself to be a house of sacrifice.... Now and for the future my eyes are open and my ears attentive to the prayer that is offered in this place. Now and for the future I have chosen consecrated this house for my name to be there for ever, my eyes and my heart will be there for ever."

PSALM 84

How lovely is your dwelling place,
Lord, God of hosts.

My soul is longing and yearning,
is yearning for the courts of the Lord.
My heart and my soul ring out their joy
to God, the living God.

The sparrow herself finds a home
and the swallow a nest for her brood,
she lays her young by your altars,
Lord of hosts, my king and my God.

They are happy, who dwell in your house,
for ever singing your praise.
They are happy, whose strength is in you,
in whose hearts are the roads to Zion.

As they go through the bitter valley
they make it a place of springs,
the autumn rain covers it with blessings.

They walk with ever growing strength,
they will see the God of gods in Zion.

O Lord God of hosts, hear my prayer
give ear, O God of Jacob.
Turn your eyes, O God, our shield,
look on the face of your anointed.

One day within your courts
is better than a thousand elsewhere.
The threshold of the house of God
I prefer to the dwellings of the wicked.

For the Lord God is a rampart, a shield,
he will give us his favor and glory.
The Lord will not refuse any good
to those who walk without blame.

Lord, God of hosts,
happy the man who trusts in you.

WRITING OF FRANCIS: 1LF 1–7

All those who love the Lord with their whole heart, with their whole soul and mind, with their whole strength (cf. Mk 12:30) and love their neighbors as themselves (cf. Mt 22:39) and hate their bodies with their vices and sins, and receive the Body and Blood of our Lord Jesus Christ, and produce worthy fruits of penance:

Oh, how happy and blessed are these men and women when they do these things and persevere in doing them, since the Spirit of the Lord will rest upon them (cf. Is 11:2) and He will make His home and dwelling among them (cf. fin 14:23). They are children of the heavenly Father (cf. Mt 5:45) whose works they do, and they are spouses, brothers, and mothers of our Lord Jesus Christ (cf. Mt 12:50).

also 1R 11:1–13

WRITING OF CLARE: RCL 12:11

Always submissive and subject at the feet of that holy Church, and steadfast in the Catholic Faith, we may observe forever the poverty and humility of our Lord Jesus Christ and of His holy Mother and the holy Gospel which we have firmly promised. Amen.

also BlCl 12

FRANCISCAN SOURCES: 1CEL 38

Truly, upon the foundation of constancy a noble structure of charity arose, in which the living stones, gathered from all parts of the world, were erected into a dwelling place of the Holy Spirit. O with what ardor of charity the new disciples of Christ burned! How great was the love that flourished in the members of this pious society! For whenever they came together anywhere, or met one another along the way, as the custom is, there a shoot of spiritual love sprang up, sprinkling over all love the seed of true affection. What more shall I say? Chaste embraces, gentle feelings, a holy kiss, pleasing conversation, modest laughter, joyous looks, a single eye, a submissive spirit, a peaceable tongue, oneness of purpose, ready obedience, unwearied hand, all these were found in them.

VATICAN II DOCUMENT: UR 2

What has revealed the love of God among us is that the only begotten Son of God has been sent by the Father into the world, so that, being made man, he might by his redemption of the entire human race give new life to it and unify it. Before offering himself up as a spotless victim upon the altar of the cross, he prayed to his Father for those who believe: "that all may be one in us, that the world may believe that you sent me" (Jn 17:21). In his Church he instituted the wonderful sacrament of the Eucharist by which the unity of the Church is both signified and brought about. He gave his followers a new commandment to love one another, and promised the Spirit, their Advocate, who, as Lord and life-giver, should remain with them forever.

After being lifted up on the cross and glorified, the Lord Jesus poured forth the Spirit whom he had promised, and through whom he has called and gathered together the people of the New Covenant, which is the Church, into a unity of faith, hope and charity, as the Apostle teaches us: "There is one body and one Spirit, just as you were called to one hope of your calling, one Lord, one faith, one baptism" (Eph 4:4–5). For "all you who have been baptized into Christ have put on Christ... for you are all one in Christ Jesus" (Gal 3:27–28). It is the Holy Spirit, dwelling in those who believe and pervading and ruling over the entire Church, who brings about that wonderful communion of the faithful and joins them together so intimately in Christ that he is the principle of the Church's unity. By distributing various kinds of spiritual gifts and ministries, he enriches the Church of Jesus Christ with different functions "in order to equip the saints for the work of service, so as to build up the body of Christ" (Eph 4: 12).

In order to establish this his holy Church everywhere in the world till the end of time, Christ entrusted to the College of the Twelve the task of teaching, ruling and sanctifying. Among their number he chose Peter. And after Peter's confession of faith, he determined that on him he would build his Church, to him he promised the keys of the kingdom of heaven, and after his profession of love, entrusted all his sheep to him to be confirmed in faith and shepherded in perfect unity, with himself, Christ Jesus, forever remaining the chief corner-stone and shepherd of our souls.

It is through the faithful preaching of the Gospel by the Apostles and their successors—the bishops with Peter's successor at their head—through their administering the sacraments, and through their governing in love, that Jesus Christ wished his people to increase, under the action of the Holy Spirit, and he perfects its fellowship in unity: in the confession of one faith, in the common celebration of divine worship, and in the fraternal harmony of the family of God.

The Church, then God's only flock, like a standard lifted on high for the nations to see it, ministers the Gospel of peace to all mankind, as it makes its pilgrim way in hope toward its goal, the fatherland above.

This is the sacred mystery of the unity of the Church, in Christ and through Christ, with the Holy Spirit energizing its various functions. The highest exemplar and source of this mystery is the unity, in the Trinity of Persons, of one God, the Father and the Son in the Holy Spirit.

PAPAL STATEMENT: EN 58

...(These communities), which come together within the

Church in order to unite themselves to the Church and to cause the Church to grow ...will be a place of evangelization, for the benefit of the bigger communities, especially the individual Churches. And, as we said at the end of the last Synod, they will be a hope for the universal Church to the extent:

◊ that they seek their nourishment in the Word of God and do not allow themselves to be ensnared by political polarization or fashionable ideologies, which are ready to explain their immense human potential:

◊ that they avoid the ever present temptation of systematic protest and a hypercritical attitude, under the pretext of authenticity and a spirit of collaboration;

◊ that they remain firmly attached to the local Church in which they are inserted, and to the universal Church, thus avoiding the very real danger of becoming isolated within themselves, then of believing themselves to be the only authentic Church of Christ, and hence of condemning the other ecclesial communities;

◊ that they maintain a sincere communion with the pastors whom the Lord has give to His Church, and with the magisterium which the Spirit of Christ has entrusted to these pastors;

◊ that they never look on themselves as the sole beneficiaries or sole agents of evangelization—or even the only depositories of the Gospel—but, being aware that the Church is much more vast and diversified, accept the fact that this Church becomes incarnate in other ways than through themselves;

◊ that they constantly grow in missionary consciousness, fervor; commitment and zeal;

◊ that they show themselves to be universal in all things and never sectarian.

On these conditions, which are certainly demanding but also uplifting, the ecclesial "communautes de base" will correspond to their most fundamental vocation: as hearers of the Gospel which is proclaimed to them and privileged beneficiaries of evangelization, they will soon become proclaimers of the Gospel themselves.

also SF 4
 EN 63
 RH 10

PRAYER: FOR THE LOCAL CHURCH

God our Father,
in all the churches scattered throughout the world
you show forth the one, holy,
      catholic and apostolic Church.
Through the gospel and the eucharist
bring your people together in the Holy Spirit
and guide us in your love.
Make us a sign of your love for all people,
and help us to show forth
the living presence of Christ in the world,
who lives and reigns with you and the Holy Spirit,
one God, for ever and ever. Amen.

Article 23

Requests for admission to the Secular Franciscan Order must be presented to the local fraternity, whose council decides upon the acceptance of new brothers and sisters.

Admission into the Order is gradually attained through a time of initiation, a period of formation of at least one year, and profession of the rule. The entire community is engaged in this process of growth by its own manner of living. The age for profession and the distinctive Franciscan sign are regulated by the statutes.

Profession by its nature is a permanent commitment.

Members who find themselves in particular difficulties should discuss their problems with the council in fraternal dialogue.

Withdrawal or permanent dismissal from the Order, if necessary, is an act of the fraternity council according to the norm of the constitutions.

THEME: THE MEANING OF COMMITMENT IN THE SECULAR FRANCISCAN ORDER

GOSPEL: MK 10:24–30

Jesus insisted, "My children," he said to them, "how hard it is to enter the kingdom of God! It is easier for a camel to pass through the eye of a needle than for a rich man to enter the kingdom of God." They were more astonished than ever. "In that case," they said to one another, "who can be saved?" Jesus gazed at them. "For men," he said, "it is impossible, but not for God: because everything is possible for God."

Peter took this up. "What about us?" he asked him. "We have left everything and followed you." Jesus said, "I tell you solemnly, there is no one who has left house, brothers, sisters, father, children or land for my sake and for the sake of the gospel who will not be repaid a hundred times over, houses, brothers, sisters, mothers, children and land—not without persecutions—now in this present time and in the world to come, eternal life."

also Lk 9:57–62

NEW TESTAMENT: HEB 10:19–25

Through the blood of Jesus we have the right to enter the sanctuary, by a new way which has opened for us, a living opening through the curtain, that is to say, his body. And we have the supreme high priest over all the house of God. So as we go in, let us be sincere in heart and filled with faith, our minds sprinkled and free from any trace of bad conscience and our bodies washed with pure water. Let us keep firm in the hope we profess, because the one who made the promise is faithful. Let us be concerned for each other, to stir a response in love and good works. Do not stay away from the meetings of the community, as some do, but encourage each other to go, the more so as you see the day drawing near.

also Cor 1:22–31

OLD TESTAMENT: DT 7:6–9

You are a people consecrated to Yahweh your God, it is you that Yahweh our God has chosen to be his very own people out of all the peoples on the earth. If Yahweh set his heart on you and chose you, it was not because you outnumbered other peoples, you were least of all peoples. It was for love of you and to keep the oath he swore to your fathers that Yahweh brought you out with his mighty hand and redeemed you from the house of slavery, from the power of Pharaoh of Egypt. Know then that Yahweh your God is God indeed, the faithful God who is true to his covenant and his graciousness for a thousand generations toward those who love him and keep his commandments.

PSALM 116B

I trusted, even when I said:
"I am sorely afflicted,"
and when I said in my alarm:
"No man can be trusted."
How can I repay the Lord
for his goodness to me?
The cup of salvation I will raise,
I will call on the Lord's name.

My vows to the Lord I will fulfill
before all his people.
O precious in the eyes of the Lord
is the death of his faithful.

Your servant, Lord, your servant am I
you have loosened my bonds.
A thanksgiving sacrifice I make:
I will call on the Lord's name.

My vows to the Lord I will fulfill
before all his people,
in the courts of the house of the Lord
in your midst, O Jerusalem.

WRITING OF FRANCIS: 1R 23:9–11

Therefore,
let us desire nothing else
let us wish for nothing else
let nothing else please us
and cause us delight
except our Creator and Redeemer and Savior,
the one true God,
Who is the Fullness of Good
    all good,
every good, the true and supreme good,
Who alone is Good
    merciful and gentle
    delectable and sweet
Who alone is holy
    just and true
    holy and right
Who alone is kind
    innocent
    pure
from Whom and through Whom is in Whom is
    all pardon
    all grace
    all glory

of all the penitent and the just
of all the blessed who rejoice together in heaven
Therefore
let nothing hinder us
nothing separate us
or nothing come between us.
Let all of us
wherever we are
in every place
at every hour
at every time of day
everyday and continually
believe and humbly
and keep in (our) heart
and love, honor, adore, serve
praise and bless
glorify and exalt
magnify and give thanks to
the most high and supreme eternal God
Trinity and Unity
the Father and the Son and the Holy Spirit
Creator of all
Savior of all who believe in Him
and hope in Him
and love Him
Who is without beginning and without end
unchangeable, invisible,
indescribable, ineffable,
incomprehensible, unfathomable,
blessed, worthy of praise,
glorious, exalted on high, sublime,
most high, gentle, lovable,
delectable and totally desirable above all else
forever.
Amen.

also LLeo 3
Test 40–41
TestCl 1–3

WRITING OF CLARE: 2L 11–14

> What you hold, may you [always] hold.
> What you do, may you [always] do and never abandon.
> But with swift pace, light step,
>   [and] unswerving feet,
>   so that even your steps stir up no dust,
> go forward
>   securely, joyfully, and swiftly,
> on the path of prudent happiness,
>   believing nothing,
>   agreeing with nothing
>   which would dussuade you from this resolution
>   or which would place a stumbling block for you on
>   the way (cf. Rom 14:13),
> so that you may offer your vows to the Most High
>   (Ps 49:14)
> in the pursuit of that perfection
> to which the Spirit of the Lord has called you.

FRANCISCAN SOURCES: 3SOC 25

Until the work of restoring the church of Saint Damian was completed, blessed Francis still wore the garments of a hermit with a strap to serve as a belt, and he carried a staff and had sandals on his feet. Then, one day during the celebration of the Mass he heard the words in which Christ bade his disciples go out and preach, carrying neither gold nor silver, nor haversack for the journey, without staff, bread, or shoes, and having no second garment. After listening to the priest's explanation of these words of the Gospel, full of unspeakable joy, he exclaimed: "this is what my whole heart desires to accomplish."

He learned these words by heart, meditating on what he had heard, and joyfully he started to put them into practice. He discarded his second garment, and from that day onwards he used no staff, shoes, or haversack, he kept one miserable tunic, and instead of the strap took a length of cord as a belt. He set his whole heart and mind on how he could best carry out the words of grace that he had heard, and, divinely inspired, he began to speak in public very simply of penitence and the life of evangelical perfection. His words were not greeted with ridicule, neither were they spoken in vain, for they possessed the strength of the Holy Spirit and went straight to the hearts of the listeners rousing them to vehement astonishment.

VATICAN II DOCUMENT: LG 44

The Christian who pledges himself to this kind of life binds himself to the practice of the three evangelical counsels by vows or by other sacred ties of a similar nature. He consecrates himself wholly to God, his supreme love. In a new and special way he makes himself over to God, to serve and honor him. True, as a baptized Christian he is dead to sin and dedicated to God, but he desires to derive still more abundant fruit from the grace of his baptism. For this purpose he makes profession in the Church of the evangelical counsels. He does so for two reasons: first, in order to be set free from hindrances that could hold him back from loving God ardently and worshipping him perfectly, and secondly, in order to consecrate himself in a more thoroughgoing way to the service of God. The bonds by which he pledges himself to the practice of the counsels show forth the unbreakable bond of union that exists between Christ and his bride the Church. The more stable and firm these bonds are, then, the more perfect will the Christian's religious consecration be.

PAPAL STATEMENT: ET 7

By a free response to the call of the Holy Spirit you have decided to follow Christ, consecrating yourselves totally to him.... (The) teaching of the Council illustrates well the grandeur of this self-giving, freely made by yourselves, after the pattern of Christ's self-giving to his Church, like his, yours is total and irreversible.... Such is your consecration, made within the Church and through her ministry—both that of her representatives who receive your profession and that of the Christian community itself, whose love recognizes, welcomes, sustains and embraces those who within it make an offering of themselves as a living sign "which can and ought to attract all the members of the Church to an effective and prompt fulfillment of the duties of their Christian vocation.... more adequately manifesting to all believers the presence of heavenly goods already possessed in this world."

PRAYER: PERPETUAL PROFESSION, A

God our Father,
you have caused the grace of baptism
to bear such fruit in your servants,
that they now strive to follow your Son more closely.
Let them rightly aim at truly evangelical perfection
and increase the holiness and apostolic zeal of your Church.
We ask this through Christ our Lord. Amen.

Article 24

To foster communion among members, the council should organize regular and frequent meetings of the community as well as meeting with other Franciscan groups, especially with youth groups. It should adopt appropriate means for growth in Franciscan and ecclesial life and encourage everyone to a life of fraternity. This communion continues with deceased brothers and sisters through prayer for them.

THEME: THE IMPORTANCE OF THE COMMUNITY GATHERING

GOSPEL: MT 18:19–20

I tell you solemnly once again, if two of you on earth agree to ask anything at all, it will be granted to you by my Father in heaven. For where two or three meet in my name, I shall be there with them.

NEW TESTAMENT: ACTS 2:42–47

These remained faithful to the teaching of the apostles, to the brotherhood, to the breaking of bread and to the prayers.

The many miracles and signs worked through the apostles made a deep impression on everyone.

The faithful all lived together and owned everything in common, they sold their goods and possessions and shared out the proceeds among themselves according to what each one needed.

They went as a body to the Temple every day but met in their houses for the breaking of bread, they shared their food gladly and generously, they praised God and were looked up to by everyone. Day by day the Lord added to their community those destined to be saved.

OLD TESTAMENT: IS 56:1, 6–8

Thus says Yahweh: Have care for justice, act with integrity, for soon my salvation will come and my integrity be manifest.

Foreigners who have attached themselves to Yahweh to serve him and to love his name and be his servants—all who observe the sabbath, not profaning it, and cling to my covenant—these I will bring to my holy mountain. I will make them joyful in my house of prayer. Their holocausts and their sacrifices will be accepted on my altar, for my house will be called a house of prayer for all the peoples.

It is the Lord Yahweh who speaks, who gathers the outcasts of Israel: there are others I will gather besides those already gathered.

PSALM 149

Sing a new song to the Lord,
his praise in the assembly of the faithful.
Let Israel rejoice in its Maker,
let Zion's sons exult in their king.
Let them praise his name with dancing
and make music with timbrel and harp.

For the Lord takes delight in his people.
He crowns the poor with salvation.
Let the faithful rejoice in their glory,
shout for joy and take their rest.
Let the praise of God be on their lips
and a two-edged sword in their hand,

to deal out vengeance to the nations
and punishment on all the peoples,
to bind their kings in chains
and their nobles in fetters of iron,
to carry out the sentence pre-ordained:
this honor is for all his faithful.

WRITING OF FRANCIS: 1R 9:10–11

And each one should confidently make known his need to the other, so that he might find what he needs and minister it to him.

And each one should love and care for his brother in all those things in which God will give him grace, as a mother loves and cares for her son.

WRITING OF CLARE: RCL 4:11–13

At least once a week the abbess is required to call her sisters together in Chapter. There both she and her sisters must confess their common and public offenses and negligences humbly. There, too, she should consult with all her sisters on whatever concerns the welfare and good of the monastery; for the Lord often reveals what is best to the lesser [among us].

FRANCISCAN SOURCES: 1CEL 39

And indeed, since they despised all earthly things and did not love themselves with a selfish love, pouring out their whole affection on all the brothers, they strove to give themselves as the price of helping one another in their needs. They came together with great desire, they remained together with joy, but separation from one another was sad on both sides, a bitter divorce, a cruel estrangement.

VATICAN II DOCUMENT: PC 15

Common life, in prayer and the sharing of the same spirit (Acts 2:42), should be constant, after the example of the early Church, in which the company of believers were of one heart and soul. It should be nourished by the teaching of the Gospel and by the sacred liturgy, especially by the Eucharist.... A community gathered together as a true family in the Lord's name enjoys his presence (cf. Mt 18:20), through the love of God which is poured into their hearts by the Holy Spirit (cf. Rom 5:5). For love sums up the law (cf. Rom 13:10) and is the bond which makes it perfect (cf. Col 3:14), by it we know that we have crossed over from death to life (cf. 1 Lk 3:14). Indeed, the unity of the brethren is a symbol of the coming of Christ (cf. Jn 13:35, 17:21) and is a source of great apostolic power.

also LG 50

PAPAL STATEMENT: EN 13

Those who sincerely accept the Good News, through the power of this acceptance and of shared faith, therefore gather together in Jesus' name in order to seek together the kingdom, build it up and live it. They make up a community which is in its turn evangelizing. The command to the Twelve to go out and proclaim the Good News is also valid for all Christians, though in a different way. It is precisely for this reason that Peter calls Christians "a people set apart to sing the praises of God," those marvelous things that each one was able to hear in his own language. Moreover, the Good News of the kingdom which is coming and which has begun is meant for all people of all times. Those who have received the Good News and who have been gathered by it into the community of salvation can and must communicate and spread it.

also EN 58

PRAYER: ELEVENTH SUNDAY IN ORDINARY TIME

God our Father,
we rejoice in the faith that draws us together,
aware that selfishness can drive us apart.
Let your encouragement be our constant strength.
Keep us one in the love that has sealed our lives
help us to live as one family
the gospel we profess.
We ask this through Christ our Lord. Amen.

Article 25

Regarding expenses necessary for the life of the fraternity and the needs of worship, of the apostolate, and of charity, all the brothers and sisters should offer a contribution according to their means. Local fraternities should contribute toward the expenses of the higher fraternity councils.

Theme: The Member's Support of the Community

Gospel: Lk 21:1–4

As he looked up he saw rich people putting their offerings into the treasury, then he happened to notice a poverty-stricken widow putting in two small coins, and he said, "I tell you truly, this poor widow has put in more than any of them, for these have all contributed money they had over, but she from the little she had has put in all she had to live on."

also Mk 12:41–44

New Testament: 2 Cor 9:1–2, 6–11

There is really no need for me to write to you on the subject of offering your services to the saints, since I know how anxious you are to help, in fact, I boast about you to the Macedonians, telling them, "Achaia has been ready since last year." So your zeal has been a spur to many more.

Do not forget: thin sowing means thin reaping; the more you sow, the more you reap. Each one should give what he had decided in his own mind, not grudgingly or because he is made to, for God loves a cheerful giver. And there is no limit to the blessings which God can send you—he will make sure that you will always have all you need for yourselves in every possible circumstance, and still have something to spare for all sorts of good works. As scripture says: He was free in almsgiving, and gave to the poor: his good deeds will never be forgotten.

The one who provides seed for the sower and bread for food will provide you with all the seed you want and make the harvest of your good deeds a larger one, and, made richer in every way, you will be able to do all the generous things which, through us, are the cause of thanksgiving to God. For doing this holy service is not only supplying all the needs of the saints, but it is also increasing the amount of thanksgiving that God receives.

OLD TESTAMENT: PROV 11:24–26

One is extravagant, yet his riches grow,
　　another excessively mean, but only grows the poorer.
The generous soul will prosper,
　　he who waters, will be watered.
The people's curse is on the man who hoards the wheat,
　　a blessing on him who sells it.

PSALM 112

Happy the man who fears the Lord,
who takes delight in all his commands.
His sons will be powerful on earth,
the children of the upright are blessed.

Riches and wealth are in his house,
his justice stands firm for ever.
He is a light in the darkness for the upright,
he is generous, merciful and just.

The good man takes pity and lends,
he conducts his affairs with honor.
The just man will never waver:
he will be remembered forever.

He has no fear of evil news,
with a firm heart he trusts in the Lord.
With a steadfast heart he will not fear
he will see the downfall of his foes.

Open-handed, he gives to the poor,
his justice stands firm for ever.

His head will be raised in glory.

The wicked man sees and is angry,
grinds his teeth and fades away,
the desire of the wicked leads to doom.

WRITING OF FRANCIS: 2R 4:2

Let the ministers and custodians alone take special care to provide for the needs of the sick and the clothing of the other brothers
through spiritual friends according to (diversity of) places and sea-
sons and cold climates, as they may judge the demands of necessity.

WRITING OF CLARE: RCL 8:7-8

Regarding the sisters who are ill, the Abbess is strictly bound to
inquire with all solicitude by herself and through other sisters what
[these sick sisters] may need both by way of counsel and of food and
other necessities and according to the resources of the place, she is
to provide for them charitably and kindly. [This is to be done]
because all are obliged to serve and provide for their sisters who are
ill just as they would wish to be served themselves if they were suffering from any infirmity.

FRANCISCAN SOURCES: 1CEL 17

Of other poor, too, while he yet remained in the world and still
followed the world, (Francis) was the helper, stretching forth a hand
of mercy to those who had nothing, and showing compassion to the
afflicted. For when one day, contrary to his custom, for he was a
most courteous person, he upbraided a certain poor man who had
asked an alms of him, he was immediately sorry, and he began to
say to himself that it was a great reproach and a shame to withhold
what was asked from one who had asked in the name of so great a
King. He therefore resolved in his heart never in the future to refuse
anyone, if at all possible, who asked for the love of God. This he most
diligently did and carried out, until he sacrificed himself entirely
and in every way, and he thus became first a practicer before he
became a teacher of the evangelical counsel: To him who asks of

thee, he said, give, and from him who would borrow of thee, do not turn away.

VATICAN II DOCUMENT: GS 65

All citizens should remember that they have the right and the duty to contribute according to their ability to the genuine progress of their own community and this must be recognized by the civil authority. Above all in areas of retarded economic progress, where all resources must be urgently exploited, the common good is seriously endangered by those who hoard their resources unproductively and by those who (apart from the case of every man's personal right of migration) deprive their community of much needed material and spiritual assistance.

PAPAL STATEMENT: PP 86

All of you who have heard the cry of the needy and are trying meet their needs are the persons we consider the promoters, and so to speak, the apostles of beneficial and genuine development which far from consisting in wealth which looks to individual advantage or is sought for its own sake, is rather to be found in an economy adjusted to the welfare of the human person and in full sustenance provided for all, the source, as it were, of fraternal charity and a clear sign of the help of Divine Providence.

PRAYER: SEVENTEENTH SUNDAY IN ORDINARY TIME

> God our Father and protector,
> without you nothing is holy,
> nothing has value.
> Guide us to use wisely
> the blessings you have given to the world.
> We ask this through Christ our Lord. Amen.

Article 26

As a concrete sign of communion and co-responsibility, the councils on various levels, in keeping with the constitutions, shall ask for suitable and well prepared religious for spiritual assistance. They should make this request to the superiors of the four religious Franciscan families, to whom the Secular Fraternity has been united for centuries.

To promote fidelity to the charism as well as observance of the rule and to receive greater support in the life of the fraternity, the minister or president, with the consent of the council, should take care to ask for a regular pastoral visit by the competent religious superiors as well as for a fraternal visit from those of the higher fraternities, according to the norm of the constitutions.

THEME: SPIRITUAL ASSISTANCE TO THE SFO COMMUNITY

GOSPEL: JN 10:11–15

> I am the good shepherd:
> the good shepherd is one who lays down his life
>   for his sheep.
> The hired man, since he is not the shepherd
> and the sheep do not belong to him,
> abandons the sheep and runs away
> as soon as he sees the wolf coming,
> and then the wolf attacks and scatters the sheep;
> this is because he is only a hired man
> and has no concern for the sheep.
> I am the good shepherd,
> I know my own
> and my own know Me,
> just as the Father knows me
> and I know the Father,
> and I lay down my life for my sheep.

also Jn 21:15–17

NEW TESTAMENT: 1 PET 4:7–11

To pray better, keep a calm and sober mind. Above all, never let your love for each other grow insincere, since love covers over many a sin. Welcome each other into your houses without grumbling. Each one of you has received a special grace, so, like good stewards responsible for all these different graces of God, put yourselves at the service of others. If you are a speaker, speak in words which seem to come from God, if you are a helper, help as though every action was done at God's orders, so that in everything God may receive the glory, through Jesus Christ, since to him alone belong all glory and power for ever and ever. Amen.

also 1 Cor 9:16–19, 22–23

OLD TESTAMENT: EZ 34:11–16

The Lord Yahweh says this: I am going to look after my flock myself and keep all of it in view. As a shepherd keeps all his flock in view when he stands up in the middle of his scattered sheep, so shall I keep my sheep in view. I shall rescue them from wherever they have been scattered during the mist and darkness, shall bring them out of the countries where they are, I shall gather them together from foreign countries and bring them back to their own land. I shall pasture them on the mountains of Israel, in the ravines and in every inhabited place in the land. I shall feed them in good pasturage, the high mountains of Israel will be their grazing ground. There they will rest in good grazing ground, they will browse in rich pastures on the mountains of Israel. I myself will pasture my sheep, I myself will show them where to rest—it is the Lord Yahweh who speaks. I shall look for the lost one, bring back the stray, bandage the wounded and make the weak strong. I shall watch over the fat and healthy. I shall be a true shepherd to them.

PSALM 121

I lift up my eyes to the mountains,
from where shall come my help?
My help shall come from the Lord
who made heaven and earth.

May he never allow you to stumble!
Let him sleep not, your guard.
No, he sleeps not nor slumbers,
Israel's guard.

The Lord is your guard and your shade,
at your right side he stands.
By day the sun shall not smite you
nor the moon in the night.

The Lord will guard you from evil,
he will guard your going and coming
both now and for ever.

WRITING OF FRANCIS: FORM LIFE 1–2

Since by divine inspiration you have made yourselves daughters and servants of the most high King, the heavenly Father, and have taken the Holy Spirit as your spouse, choosing to live according to the perfection of the holy Gospel, I resolve and promise for myself and for my brothers always to have that same loving care and special solicitude for you as (I have) for them.

also LLeo 4

WRITING OF CLARE: RCL 12:1–6

Our Visitor, according to the will and command of our Cardinal, should always be taken from the Order of Friars Minor. He should be the kind of person who is well known for his virtue and good life. It shall be his duty to correct any excesses against the form of our profession, whether these be in the leadership or among the members. Taking his stand in a public place, so that he can be seen by others, he may speak with several in a group and with individuals about the things that pertain to the duty of visitation, as it may seem best to him.

With respect for the love of God and of Blessed Francis we ask as a favor from the Order of Friars Minor a chaplain and a clerical companion of good character and reputation and prudent discretion, and two lay brothers who are lovers of holiness of life and virtue, to support us in our [life of] poverty, just as we have always had [them] through the kindness of the Order.

FRANCISCAN SOURCES: SF 73

Francis, the faithful servant and perfect imitator of Christ, feeling himself wholly united to Christ through the virtue of holy humility, desired this humility in his friars before all other virtues. And in order that they might love, desire, acquire, and preserve it, he gave them constant encouragement by his own example and teaching, and particularly impressed this on the ministers and preachers, urging them to undertake humble tasks.

He used to say that they must not allow the duties of high office or the responsibility of preaching to stand in the way of holy and devout prayer, going out for alms, doing manual labor when required, and carrying out other humble duties like the rest of the brethren, both as a good example and for good of their own and others' souls. He said, "The friars under obedience are much edified when their ministers and preachers gladly devote their time to prayer, and apply themselves to humble and undistinguished tasks. Unless they do this they cannot admonish other friars without embarrassment, injustice, and self-condemnation, for if we follow Christ's example, we must act rather than teach, and our acting and teaching must go together."

VATICAN II DOCUMENT: PO 9

Even though the priests of the new law by reason of the sacrament of Order fulfill the preeminent and essential function of father and teacher among the people of God and on their behalf, still they are disciples of the Lord along with all the faithful and have been made partakers of his kingdom by God, who has called them by his grace. Priests, in common with all who have been reborn in the font of baptism, are brothers among brothers as members of the same Body of Christ which all are commanded to build up.

Priests should, therefore, occupy their position of leadership as men who do not seek the things that are their own but the things that are Jesus Christ's. They should unite their efforts with those of the lay faithful and conduct themselves among them after the example of the Master who came amongst men "not to be served but to serve, and to live his life as a ransom for many" (Mt 20:28). Priests are to be sincere in this appreciation and promotion of lay people's dignity and of the special role the laity have to play in the Church's mission. They should also have an unfailing respect for the just liberty which belongs to everybody in civil society. They should be willing to listen to lay people, give brotherly consideration to their wishes, and recognize their experience and competence in the different fields of human activity. In this way they will be able to recognize along with them the signs of the times.

While trying the spirits if they be of God, they must discover faith, recognize with joy and foster with diligence the many and varied charismatic gifts of the laity, whether these be of a humble or more exalted kind. Among the other gifts of God which are found abundantly among the faithful, special attention ought to be devoted to those graces by which a considerable number of people are attracted to greater heights of the spiritual life. Priests should also be confident in giving lay people charge of duties in the service of the Church, giving them freedom and opportunity for activity and even inviting them, when opportunity occurs, to take the initiative in undertaking projects of their own.

Finally, priests have been placed in the midst of the laity so that they may lead them to the unity of charity, "loving one another with brotherly affection: outdoing one another in sharing honor" (Rom 12:10). Theirs is the task, then, of bringing about agreement amongst divergent outlooks in such a way that nobody may feel a stranger in the Christian community. They are to be at once the defenders of the common good, for which they are responsible in the bishop's name, and at the same time the unwavering champion of truth lest the faithful be carried about with every wind of doctrine. Those who have abandoned the practice of the sacraments, or even perhaps the faith, are entrusted to priests as special objects of their care. They will not neglect to approach these as good shepherds.

Priests should keep in mind what has been laid down in regard to ecumenism and not forget those fellow Christians who do not enjoy complete ecclesiastical union with us.

They will regard as committed to their charge all those who fail to recognize Christ as their Savior.

The faithful for their part ought to realize that they have obligations to their priests. They should treat them with filial love as being their fathers and pastors. They should also share their priests' anxieties and help them as far as possible by prayer and active work so that they may be better able to overcome difficulties and carry out their duties with greater success.

also AA 25

PAPAL STATEMENT: EN 68

A mark of our identity, which no doubt ought to encroach upon and no objection eclipse, is this: as pastors, we have been chosen by the mercy of the Supreme Pastor, in spite of our inadequacy, to proclaim the Word of God, to assemble the scattered People of God, to feed this People with the signs of the action of Christ which are the sacraments, to set this People on the road to salvation, to maintain it in that unity of which we are, at different levels, active and living instruments, and unceasingly to keep this community gathered around Christ faithful to its deepest vocation. And when we do all these things, within our human limits and by grace of God, it is a work of evangelization that we are carrying out.

PRAYER: FOR THE MINISTERS OF THE CHURCH

Father,
you have taught the ministers of your Church
not to desire that they be served but to serve
    their brothers
and sisters.
May they be effective in their work
and persevering in their prayer,
performing their ministry with gentleness and
    concern for others.
We ask this through Christ our Lord. Amen.

Conclusion:

"May whoever observes all this be filled in heaven with the blessing of the most high Father, and on earth with that of his beloved Son, together with the Holy Spirit, the Comforter."

Blessing of St. Francis from the *Testament*

THEME: THE BLESSING OF FAITHFULNESS

GOSPEL: LK 11:27–28

Now as Jesus was speaking, a woman in the crowd raised her voice and said, "Happy the womb that bore you and the breasts you sucked!" But he replied, "Still happier those who hear the word of God and keep it."

also Mt 10:22 & 24:13

NEW TESTAMENT: REV 14:13

Then I heard a voice from heaven say to me. "Write down: Happy are those who die in the Lord! Happy indeed, the Spirit says; now they can rest for ever after their work, since their good deeds go with them."

OLD TESTAMENT: NEH 9:7–8

Yahweh, you are the God who chose Abram, brought him out from Ur in Chaldea, and gave him the name of Abraham. Finding him faithful of heart before you, you made a covenant with him. And you kept your promise because you are just.

PSALM 24

The Lord's is the earth and its fullness,
the world and all its peoples.
It is he who set it on the seas;
on the waters he made it firm.

Who shall climb the mountain of the Lord?
What shall stand in his holy place?
The man with clean hands and pure heart,
who desires not worthless things,
who has not sworn so as to deceive his neighbor.

He shall receive blessings from the Lord
and reward from the God who saves him.
Such are the men who seek him,
seek the face of the God of Jacob.

WRITING OF FRANCIS: 2LF 86–88

In the name of the Father and of the Son and of the Holy Spirit. Amen. I, Brother Francis, your little servant, ask and implore you in the love which is God (cf. 1 Jn 4:16) and with the desire to kiss your feet, to receive these words and others of our Lord Jesus Christ with humility and love, and observe them and put them into practice. And to all men and women who will receive them kindly and understand their meaning and pass them on to others by the example: If they have persevered in them to the end (Mt 24:13), may the Father and the Son and the Holy Spirit bless them. Amen.

WRITING OF CLARE: 1L 31–32

I have resolved to beg [you] by my humble prayers in the mercy of Christ, to be strengthened in His holy service, and to progress from good to better, from virtue to virtue, so that He whom you serve with the total desire of your soul may bestow on you the reward for which you long.

FRANCISCAN SOURCES: LP 43B

One night, as Francis was thinking of all the tribulations he was enduring, he felt sorry for himself and said interiorly: "Lord, help me in my infirmities, so that I may have the strength to bear them patiently!" And suddenly he heard a voice in spirit: "Tell me, Brother: if, in compensation for your sufferings and tribulations you were given an immense and precious treasure: the whole mass of the earth changed into pure gold, pebbles into precious stones, and the water of the rivers into perfume, would you not regard the pebbles and the waters as nothing compared to such a treasure? Would you not rejoice?" Blessed Francis answered: "Lord, it would be a very great, very precious, and inestimable treasure beyond all that one can love and desire!" "Well, Brother," the voice said, "be glad and joyful in the midst of your infirmities and tribulations: as of now, live in peace as if you were already sharing my kingdom."

also 2 Cel 213

Vatican II Document: LG 47

Let everyone who has been called to the profession of the [evangelical] counsels take earnest care to preserve and excel still more in the life in which God has called him, for the increase of the holiness of the Church, to the greater glory of the one and undivided Trinity, which in Christ and through Christ is the source and origin of all holiness.

Papal Statement: RD 17

Beloved Brothers and Sisters! "God is faithful, by whom you were called into the fellowship of his Son, Jesus Christ our Lord" (1 Cor 1:9). Persevering in fidelity to him who is faithful, strive to find a very special support in Mary! For she was called by God to the most perfect communion with his Son. May she, the faithful Virgin, also be the Mother of your evangelical way: may she help you to experience and to show to the world how infinitely faithful is God himself!

Prayer: First Religious Profession

Lord,
you have inspired our brothers and sisters
with the resolve to follow Christ more closely.
Grant a blessed ending to the journey
on which they have set out,
so that they may be able to offer you
the perfect gift of their loving service.
We ask this through Christ our Lord. Amen.

Bibliography

ϯ SCRIPTURE:

The Jerusalem Bible. Garden City NY: Doubleday and Company, Inc., 1966.

PSALMS:

The Grail Psalmody. London: & Collins Son & Co Ltd. 7 1966.
http://giamusic.com

WRITINGS OF ST. FRANCIS AND OF ST. CLARE:

Armstrong OFMCap, Regis J., and Brady OFM, Ignatius C. *Francis and Clare: The Complete Works.* New York: Paulist Press, 1982.
http://www.paulistpress.com

FRANCISCAN SOURCES:

Habig OFM, Marian A. (editor). *St. Francis of Assisi, Sources.* Chicago: Franciscan Herald Press, 1973.

VATICAN II DOCUMENTS:

Flannery OP, Austin (editor). *Vatican Council II: The Conciliar and Post Conciliar Documents.* Dublin: Dominican Publications 1975.

Documents of Vatican Council II:

http://www.vatican.va/archive/hist_councils/ii_vatican_council/
http://www.rc.net/rcchurch/vatican2/
http://www.con.org/vatiidoc.hltml/

Papal Statements:

http://www.vatican.va/holy_father/

Pope John XXIII. *Pacem in Terris*. Washington: National Catholic Welfare Conference, 11 April 1963.

Pope Paul VI. *Ecclesiam Suam (Paths of the Church)*. Washington: National Catholic Welfare Conference, 6 August 1964.

_____. *Populorum Progressio (On the Development of Peoples)*. Washington: United States Catholic Conference, 26 March 1967.

_____. *Evangelii Nuntiandi (On Evangelization in the Modern World)*. New York: Daughters of St. Paul, 8 December 1975.

Pope John Paul I. *Address to Group of Visiting U.S. Bishops*. Washington: United States Catholic Conference, 21 September 1978.

Pope John Paul II. *A Call to Fidelity: Homily given during Eucharistic Celebration in Cathedral of the Assumption, Mexico City*. Washington: United States Catholic Conference, 26 January 1979.

_____. *Redemptor Hominis (Redeemer of Man)*. Washington: United States Catholic Conference, 4 March 1979.

_____. *Dives in Misericordia (On the Mercy of God)*. Rome: Vatican Polyglot Press, 30 November 1980.

_____. *Laborem Exercens (On Human Work)*. Rome: Vatican Polyglot Press, 14 September 1981.

_____. *Familiaris Consortio (Christian Family in the Modern World)*. London: Catholic Truth Society, 22 November 1981.

_____. "Studiate, amate, vivete la regola dell'Ordine Francescano Secolare." Roma: *L'Osservatore Romano*, 28 September 1982, translation by Adalbert Wolski TOR.

_____. *Salvifici Doloris (On the Christian Meaning of Human Suffering)*. Rome: Vatican Polyglot Press, 11 February 1984.

_____. *Redemptionis Donum (On Religious Consecration)*. Rome: Vatican Polyglot Press, 25 March 1984.

_____. *Reconciliatio et Paenitentia (On Reconciliation and Penance in the Mission of the Church Today)*. Rome: Vatican Polyglot Press, 2 December 1984.

PRAYERS:

The Roman Missal: The Sacramentary. New York: Catholic Book
Publishing Co., 1985.

Index

181